Speaking Personally

Journalism: Reflections on Practice

Series Editors: **Julian Petley**, Professor of Screen Media, Brunel University, UK; **Sarah Niblock**, Professor and Head of Journalism, Brunel University, UK

This series provides journalists, academics and students with a unique practical and critical guide to key areas of contemporary journalism practice for the digital age. Each volume offers a local and global perspective, with digital aspects considered throughout. The first series to really synthesise theory with practice, these books will both demonstrate how real-world journalists navigate and accommodate everyday demands, challenges and opportunities in the industry and teach us how to reflect on this.

Published titles:

James Rodgers
REPORTING CONFLICT

Murray Dick
SEARCH: THEORY AND PRACTICE IN JOURNALISM ONLINE

Rosalind Coward
SPEAKING PERSONALLY

For more information on titles in the series, please visit www.palgrave.com/media/jrp

---

Series standing order
Series ISBN: 978–0–230–58080–0

If you would like to receive future titles in this series as they are published, you can make use of our standing order facility. To place a standing order please contact your bookseller or, in case of difficulty, write to us at the address below with your name and address and the name of the series. Please state with which title you wish to begin your standing order.

Customer Services Department, Macmillan Distribution Ltd, Houndmills, Basingstoke, Hampshire, RG21 6XS, UK

Speaking Personally

The Rise of Subjective and Confessional Journalism

By Rosalind Coward

palgrave
macmillan

First published 2013 by
PALGRAVE MACMILLAN

Palgrave Macmillan in the UK is an imprint of Macmillan Publishers Limited,
registered in England, company number 785998, of Houndmills, Basingstoke,
Hampshire RG21 6XS.

Palgrave Macmillan in the US is a division of St Martin's Press LLC,
175 Fifth Avenue, New York, NY 10010.

Palgrave Macmillan is the global academic imprint of the above companies
and has companies and representatives throughout the world.

Palgrave® and Macmillan® are registered trademarks in the United States,
the United Kingdom, Europe and other countries.

ISBN 978–0–230–36020–4 paperback

This book is printed on paper suitable for recycling and made from fully
managed and sustained forest sources. Logging, pulping and manufacturing
processes are expected to conform to the environmental regulations of the
country of origin.

A catalogue record for this book is available from the British Library.

A catalog record for this book is available from the Library of Congress.

Contents

Acknowledgements   vi

Introduction   1
1   The Impersonal Voice and the Fallacies of Objectivity   13
2   Changing Places: Opinion Columns and Editorials   32
3   Gonzo and I: The New Journalism   52
4   Getting Closer: Feminisation, Featurisation and the
    Confessional Society   70
5   Confessional Journalism   91
6   Blogging and the Intimate Universality of Cyberspace   113
Conclusion   134

Bibliography   141

Index   148

Acknowledgements

A number of people and institutions have been instrumental in helping this book see the light of day.

At the forefront is Sarah Niblock, the series editor. Without her generous encouragement, patience, support and loyal friendship, this book would never have happened.

The Annenberg Institute at the University of Pennsylvania housed me as a research associate for a semester and gave me access to their resources. I am very grateful for this opportunity, and I am particularly grateful to Barbie Zelizer who arranged this and was supportive throughout. Carolyn Marvin and Katherine Sender gave me valuable encouragement and perceptive feedback.

Paul Sutton, my Head of Department at Roehampton University, has been a source of constant support, and I am extremely grateful to him for his generous spirit and encouragement. I am grateful to Roehampton University for supporting my research.

Various friends and colleagues have in a variety of ways – some they may not even know about – helped me with this project with useful information, timely encouragement and access to resources. These include Ann Mc Ferran, Susan Greenberg, Nicci Gerrard, Yasmin Alibhai-Brown, Becky Gardiner and Sally Weale. I am extremely grateful also to Peter Preston for his readiness to answer all questions so promptly, so patiently and so informatively. None of these people bear any responsibility for the ideas advanced here.

Finally my thanks go to my partner, John Ellis, who, as always, has provided endless encouragement, practical support and intellectual input.

Introduction

Contemporary journalism is full of people 'speaking personally'. Whether it is opinion pieces written by vivid personalities, articles based on first-person real-life experiences, magazines addressing their readers in intimate terms, confessional columns detailing intimate life experiences or blogs on Internet sites, the personal voice is everywhere. This book is an exploration of how and why personal voices, which also frequently tell personal stories, have come to play such an important role in journalism. Appropriately this exploration starts with a story.

The date is April 2009. The world is in the grip of fears about swine flu. A young Scottish couple, Dawn and Iain Askham, have just returned to Glasgow from their honeymoon in Mexico. Although Mexico has been identified as the epicentre of the illness and talk is of a possible global pandemic, the Askhams have been cut off from world news enjoying 'a holiday of a lifetime'. Back home, they resume their normal lives, paying scant attention to the coughs and sneezes they develop. But Dawn's mother has been following the media coverage of swine flu. When the couple begin to feel worse, she calls a doctor.

Suddenly Dawn and Iain find themselves at the centre of a major health alert. When the doctor realises they have been in Mexico, they are taken by an ambulance to a hospital where they are quarantined. Their contacts are put under scrutiny and 48 hours later one of Iain's pub chums, Graeme, is confirmed as having the virus strain H1N1, known as swine flu. Dawn and Iain, now feeling pretty ill themselves, are suddenly at the epicentre of a scenario everyone has been dreading. Not only have they become the first confirmed cases in the United Kingdom, but they appear to be responsible for the first confirmed transmission of the illness, human to human.

It's a scary time for the couple. The tabloid press is in a state of hysteria and no one really knows how serious the virus is. It is known to have killed many in Mexico, but when Dawn and Iain fell ill, no one outside that country had died with the illness. Both of them are feeling ill and worried about how the other is faring in isolation. Eventually they begin to recover slowly, but there's no call for celebration. They are assailed by doubts and anxieties: relief at being alive but guilt too, at possibly having triggered a UK epidemic. Gradually though, they realise with amazement, they – and their friends – have survived a disease so many have feared. The worst has not happened. Emerging from hospital, what joy, what thankfulness, what bewilderment they must be feeling.

If Dawn and Iain had survived a similar experience in any previous century, it is likely that, awash with such feelings, they would have headed straight to church. They might have fallen on their knees and thanked God, or the local saint, for their survival. Perhaps they would have prayed earnestly in church to avert any further disaster befalling themselves or their family. Maybe the experience would have changed their lives for good. They had escaped death, so perhaps they would now devote themselves to some good cause in gratitude or donate some portion of their income to some deserving cause. But this is the twenty-first century and this is Britain. There are a lot of people out there interested in this story and what it felt like to be in the centre of it all. So what do Dawn and Iain do? They make contact with Max Clifford, publicity guru, to sell their story to the media.

Now instead of the priest or God hearing their confessions, it's the *Daily Mail* which receives them, doubtless in return for a decent fee (*The Daily Mail* 1 May 2009). The newspaper wants to know not only what happened, but particularly how they felt about this experience. Dawn and Iain oblige, telling the newspapers all about their symptoms and then in great detail about their personal feelings. The Askhams add that they are deeply grateful to the National Health Service and the health workers who looked after them. For a moment, there's a glimpse of the puppet master pulling some strings here. This is a very Max Clifford touch. Clifford, one of the most powerful figures in the British media is often found behind stories of ordinary people in the British tabloids, and he is very keen on the NHS, because it looked after his daughter who was born with chronic arthritis. Clifford would like this story because it's an opportunity to speak positively about the health service.

One or two commentators shake their heads over Clifford 'managing' the couple's story. But the press doesn't turn against them unlike another couple in the press's glare at the same time. The parents of the abducted three-year-old Madeleine McCann who went missing in Portugal in May 2007 were thought by some journalists not to be reacting 'appropriately' (Bainbridge 2009). Madeleine's mother, Kate, in particular had remained cool and not poured out her heart to the press. Consequently she received increasingly hostile press coverage. Deprived of revelations given willingly, the press helped themselves. The *News of the World* published Kate McCann's diary without her permission, a diary detailing her agony when Madeleine disappeared. Later, this desperation for the intimacies of Kate McCann became one of the many shocking stories addressed by the Leveson Inquiry (2011).

But at the time, no one seemed to think there was much wrong with Dawn and Ian selling their story. Nor would Clifford much care if anyone did, although he likes people to know he's driven by a sort of personal morality. He likes to tell how he'll only handle stories if he believes in them or there's some chemistry between himself and the person concerned. Moreover, he has a defence: he likes to present himself as champion of ordinary people who get caught up in the media. 'If it's your story, and the media are going to make money from your story', says Clifford, 'why shouldn't you make money from your story?' (BBC 1 May 2009).

'Your story.' These words could be the leitmotif of today's media, the words written through the stick of the media rock, found wherever you bite into it. In today's journalism, a report about the swine flu couple is insufficient. We want their real-life experience with all details, especially all the emotions and feelings straight from the protagonists' mouths. 'Your story' is the mark of a story's authenticity – the real person telling the real story with the authentic feeling.

Such stories – detailing intimacies and especially difficult situations and personal reactions to them – are staple fare of contemporary journalism (and the media as a whole). Because some newspapers are prepared to pay for exclusive rights to particular stories, and because ordinary people can become celebrities through this process, there's sometimes money to be made. That's why people are prepared to sell them, that's why journalists have been prepared to break the law sometimes to get them and that's why PR agents like Max Clifford can make a business of it. Indeed, at the same time as the bird flu scare, he was in the thick of controversy around another client's story. Jade Goody, who died of cervical cancer in March that same year, had willingly exposed intimate and increasingly graphic details of her illness. Her story not only attracted huge coverage but also provoked widespread debate about self-exposure in the media. Some valued her revelations: they encouraged other young women to get cancer check-ups. Others were appalled, branding it exploitation, although opinion divided over whether she was exploiting the public or being exploited herself.

By strange coincidence, these same issues – manipulation, exploitation, self-exposure – were at the centre of yet another simultaneous media scandal. Again the ethics of self-exposure were central. But this time instead of journalists harvesting – and possibly exploiting – other people's personal stories, it was journalists telling their own personal stories and exploiting their own families. In March 2009, journalist Julie Myerson found herself at the centre of controversy about using her son for copy. The controversy followed publication of her non-fiction book, *The Lost Child* (Myerson 2009), ostensibly about a girl born in Victorian times who died young of TB. Myerson had interwoven the tale of this lost child with a more personal element, an account of her estrangement from another lost child, her son, Jake. She had evicted him from the family home after a violent fight during which her eardrum was perforated. Jake, she claimed, was 'lost' to drugs. Within days of the first publicity, the story blew up in the media with commentators appalled about exposing a teenage boy in this way. Minette Marrin (*Sunday Times* 8 March 2009) called it a 'betrayal not just of love and intimacy, but also of motherhood itself'. Tim Lott wrote 'Julie has betrayed Jake for her own ambition' (*The Independent* 8 March 2009).

Myerson was widely interviewed in British broadsheets explaining she had been motivated to write this book to 'help others', whose children had been 'claimed' by skunk. Meanwhile her son Jake was easily traced via his Facebook page by the tabloids and gave some bitter interviews himself. It made painful reading and views polarised. Myerson was either brave for publicising such an important issue or she was self-indulgent – and cruel – for exposing her son's troubles without his permission, possibly damaging his chances of recovery by publicly humiliating him. This latter view gained currency when it emerged that *The Lost Child* was not a 'one-off' but another output from a writer who had already made liberal use of her own life and family in her journalism. It soon emerged that Julie Myerson was also the author of the *Saturday Guardian*'s anonymous column 'Living with Teenagers', which had ended abruptly a few months earlier when the teenagers in question discovered not only that they had been the subject of this revealing column but also that all their school friends and their parents had guessed this already. After the *Guardian* confirmed Julie Myerson had been the series' author, it removed the articles from its website to 'protect their privacy' (*The Guardian* 10 March 2009).

This controversy had particular resonance for me. For two years, I had written a column which sat alongside Julie Myerson's in the 'Family' section of the *Saturday Guardian*. The column, 'Looking after Mother', which ran in the *Guardian* between 2006 and 2008 was about my mother, who had developed dementia, and whose care I was mainly responsible for. The column, published under my own name, tracked the daily experiences of caring for someone in this condition as she continued to try and live independently. It was about the pain of watching my mother's decline, about the difficulties of the unrecognised work of caring for someone in this condition and about the struggles with doctors, hospitals and social workers. But it was also about the many humourous occasions which arose with someone as spirited as my mother. It seemed to sit well beside Julie Myerson's column, two ends of women's domestic lives.

However, during the period of writing, I often vacillated myself between the two dominant responses to Julie Myerson's book. It felt important to tell the story of what life was really like for people with dementia and their carers. It was after all a subject which was swept under the carpet, but now affecting increasing numbers. I told myself it was important journalism on par with more conventional campaigning and investigative journalism, but raising issues in more personal and empathetic ways. Readers of the column tended to support this. The column, they said, made them feel they were not alone with their difficulties, and they appreciated having their own experiences with elderly dependents reflected back to them. Nevertheless I had dilemmas about how much of my life to expose and doubts about the ethics of exposing the life of someone else who was still alive and who had no real control over the representations. As I wrote in one column, I never really knew how much my mother actually consented since, in her condition; it was difficult to give full consent. I once received a letter – was it from someone who knew my mother? – saying, 'How dare I write about somebody else's life like this?' The letter claimed I was abusing her privacy. Although it was the one critical voice among much appreciation, it was the one I often dwelt on.

In my own case, after two years, I decided to finish writing this column writing 'If I continued, it would be increasingly with the indignities and decline. Mum herself does not really seem to mind. "No, no", she said the other night, "write what you like. I'd like to find out about myself". But not everyone in my family has seen it that way and I've met some opposition for "invading her privacy". I know there are greater difficulties ahead, decisions we will have to take about how she is looked after, how we deal with decline, and sadly there will probably be more family conflict. While I genuinely believe it has been, and would continue to be, a good thing to explore this publicly – because these issues affect so many people now – simultaneously I know that to continue would not leave open the possibility of healing family division' (*The Guardian* 18 October 2008).

I had run up against the dilemmas facing journalists writing about their own lives, dilemmas which erupted around Julie Myerson. These sorts of columns are not (at least ostensibly) fiction. They are about real people: the writers and the protagonists in the columns. Writers, like Julie Myerson, and me, are professionals, earning money from these stories and we have professional strategies for dealing with personal revelations. But our subjects – mothers, lovers and children – have not necessarily given consent, or have given consent that they do not fully understand. Nor do they necessarily benefit from their exposure. Sometimes they are people in direct conflict with the writers and their version of events, as Jake Myerson was at that time. How much right does an autobiographical journalist have to include material of living members of family, especially if there is a background of conflict or dispute? Whose life is it anyway?

Provoked by the dilemmas of my 'Looking after Mother' column, I began thinking about 'speaking personally' in the press. I hadn't always written this kind of intimate journalism although my journalism had often contained personal experience for reasons which will be explored in Chapter 4. Over the years, however, this personal writing had become increasingly prominent and I recognised that in producing this kind of copy I belonged to a wider trend. Personal pieces and first-person real-life stories have become ever more abundant, either written by the protagonists themselves or 'as told to' journalists. Features have become more intimate and confessional while even news stories now include many personal stories. All journalists are aware of the pressure to humanise stories by including more personal and intimate experiences including self-revelations. Simultaneously, there has been a huge increase in autobiographical journalism including numerous columns ranging from lightweight personal diaries like Tim Dowling's in the *Guardian* to John Diamond's account of his cancer in the *Times* between 1997 and 2001.

This trend towards more personal material shows up in other ways too. There has been an increase in personality-based journalism, as well as an explosion of opinion-led journalism where often the personalities of the writers are much more ostentatiously on view. The personal lives of writers are also more up front while personal viewpoint is more blatant even in political commentary. This is not confined to tabloids. One British 'quality' newspaper, the *Independent*, rebranded itself as a 'viewspaper' while the *Times* and the *Guardian* both employ highly personal commentators and flamboyant personalities such as David Mitchell and Mariella Frostrup. On the Internet, the personal voice is king whether it is intimate confessions of personal bloggers or the blatantly opinionated views in blogs. The Huffington Post, whose success took conventional newspapers by surprise (Rusbridger 2006), is all about the strong personal voice, whether in the emphatic viewpoints encouraged in its commentary or in its regular lifestyle blogs. In this respect, it mirrors the direct personal address and intimacy of social networking and online communities and has been very influential as conventional newspapers redefine themselves online.

Speaking personally is now a dominant element in journalism and core to the practices of journalism on the Internet, but there's virtually nothing about it when it comes to critical dialogue, analysis, reflection and debate, either among journalists or in academia. Anyone like me hoping to glean any ethical guidance about this kind of writing would hope in vain. Personal writing is barely acknowledged as journalism in many quarters. Its ethical dilemmas are not regarded as journalism's most pressing issues. Nor is information to be found about its history – where it came from, why it found such a ready home in journalism and what – if any – are its conventions and parameters.

This lack is particularly noticeable in academia. At the beginning of most university journalism courses, tutors start with a drumroll question: 'what is journalism?' The first answers given by students are remarkably consistent. They invariably mention 'reporting' on 'facts'. Often in that first lecture of that first term, tutors reinforce this first answer using something like Brian McNair's definition as a working premise. Journalism is 'any authored text, in written, audio or visual form, which claims to be (i.e. is presented to its audience as) a truthful statement about, or record of some hitherto unknown (new) feature of the actual, social world' (1998, p. 4). As the course progresses, tutors may deconstruct this definition, problematising, as McNair himself encourages, notions like 'truthful statement'. They will almost certainly point out how McNair has qualified his views, suggesting that the text 'is presented' to the audience rather than 'is' a truthful statement. And they will also likely suggest that journalism itself often fails to live up to the ideals implicit here; sometimes being neither truthful nor accurate.

In short, tutors will explore McNair's warning that his definition invites more questions than it gives answers. But few will reject out of hand the statement's implicit aspirations: that journalism should be, if it could be, a truthful and accurate record of actual social events. Even when tutors lead students to reflect philosophically on whether journalism can ever accurately portray 'the truth' or indeed whether 'truth' exists as such, most will still teach students how to write in ways which will enable 'objective', 'accurate' reporting of real events.

Trainee journalists will learn conventions and techniques about reporting 'impartially' and communicating 'objectively'. These will be all about excluding subjectivity. Journalists, they will be told, should be a conduit to events, not get in the way of them. Implicitly they will also learn that there are some subjects which are serious – politics, world events, disasters and social trends – and some that are trivial – personal feelings.

All the personal writing mentioned earlier departs in content and style from these common-sense notions of journalism. Not only is most of it openly subjective, but it is also often partisan. Often it deals with what appears trivial, preoccupied with small-scale events, with intimate, domestic matters, the inner emotional life, the opposite of subjects considered proper journalism.

When professionals and academics do address subjective journalism, it is invariably as a problem. Debates about the quality of British journalism are full of anxiety about 'dumbing down', 'trivialisation' and 'sensationalism'. Closer examination reveals that behind these worries is the spectre of increasingly subjective viewpoints. The thesis runs that objective, fact-based knowledgeable reportage has given way to sensationalist, partisan and trivial concerns not just in the tabloids but also in the broadsheets. Typically Peter Wilby (*New Statesman* 13 March 2006) bemoans 'the rise of a commentariat who express opinions that have no basis in knowledge'. The growth of the Internet has inflamed these worries. When people turn away from conventional news outlets to other sources information – social networks, blogs and online communities – they are turning to outlets which characteristically foreground subjectivity and personal opinion. Many critics fear that not only is the Internet undercutting the commercial viability of traditional journalistic outlets, since newspapers have not yet found ways of making their presence on the web profitable, but also that objective, accurate and dispassionate reporting is being replaced by an unregulated, multi-sourced, citizen-led media dominated by opinionated and partisan journalism. 'There is no oracle now', said Hugo Young (2003), 'only a cacophony of rival voices'.

There are good reasons for anxiety about the state of the press. If journalism is one of the key ways in which citizens are informed about society allowing them to participate fully as citizens in a democracy, then the lack of money to invest in high-quality, well-researched, accurate journalism is a genuine worry. But the threat to these cannot simply be laid at the door of more personal journalism. The real threat is because it is becoming increasingly difficult to maintain the traditional regulated outlets, which are expensive, at a time when information can be found for free on the Internet. That readers or consumers are attracted to – and engaged by – a journalism which is more subjective and transparent should be pause for thought rather than seen as the cause of establishment journalism's demise.

This question of the popularity of personal, opinionated journalism is one good reason to bring this type of writing into full critical view. Why does it have the power to pull in audiences when other forms of journalism are flagging? Traditional news and reportage is losing audiences not just because of changes in patterns of consumption brought about by the Internet. The decline is also because audiences find blogs, personal columns and more transparently personal stories more engaging than traditional journalism. If they wanted to, young consumers could watch news 24 hours a day. But they don't. The new generation is turning towards different, more personalised forms of communication, where they can get access to groups with shared interest, argue directly with opinions when they encounter them, engage with personalities who interest them and explore intimate themes of relationships, emotions and health when they need to. Arguably this kind of journalism connects people to public debates more effectively than the old sources of information.

A connected reason for paying this personal journalism more attention is that it can be extraordinarily powerful. We have only to think of John Diamond's column tracing his struggle with cancer which enabled people to talk more openly about the big 'C', or Joan Didion's extraordinary dissection of personal grief in *The Year of Magical Thinking* (Didion 2005), or Mathew Engel's heartbreaking account of losing his beloved son, 'The Day the Sky Fell In' (*The Guardian* 3 December 2005), or 'The Wave: A Tragedy in Mexico', journalist Francisco Goldman's devastating account of fate and guilt after his wife drowned (*New Yorker* 7 February 2011). As this book will argue, these are the pieces of journalism we remember and cherish, the writing which helps us through our own journeys and dilemmas. This kind of writing widens the reach of journalism and humanises it.

When I first started in journalism, many of these 'emotional' issues were regarded as private, not relevant to news agenda. Not so long ago such issues would have included cancer, rape, abortion or depression, all now considered absolutely central social issues. It was the personal accounts that made the public realise the consequences of these conditions – and indeed sometimes also their causes. There is an honourable tradition where journalists have tackled subjects considered private and off-limits, while making clear their personal investment in such issues, and in so doing have created some of the best journalism there is and changed social attitudes. Journalist Jill Tweedie's championing of the issue of domestic violence against women in the *Guardian* in the 1970s comes to mind.

Journalism where a writer's personality, reactions and beliefs are visible is not new. Some of the greatest pieces of journalism and reportage have been those where the personal voice is heard most clearly whether as advocate, confidante or even reporter, as this book will argue. But it is true that personal journalism has mushroomed recently and must be seen in a wider social context – the confessional society. On television, in books, and on the Internet, there is a fascination with 'your story' – personal experiences, stories and reactions. The raison d'etre of reality television is scrutinising people's lives, dilemmas and reactions to difficult situations (Ellis 2007). Far from being trivial and irrelevant, personal revelations are part of the zeitgeist.

A number of influential sociologists (Giddens 1991, Bauman 2001, Beck and Beck-Gernsheim 2001) have suggested that a key characteristic of late modernity is the requirement for individuals to define and refine their identities reflexively. Whereas traditional society ascribed people roles in which they often remained for life, late modernity is premised on people finding, creating or exploring subjectivity – their own and others. The increasing interest in personal revelations and memoirs is part of this exploration of subjectivities which are no longer fixed but up for grabs. Self-revelation and scrutiny of others' intimacies is about witnessing others create themselves and respond to ethical dilemmas. We need real-life stories to witness and thereby to test ourselves. It is as if in a culture which is no longer under strict moral instructions from traditional authorities – the church, parents, the state – we are asking not how *should* we react, but how *would* we react?

Most newspapers have implicitly recognised the importance of more personal writing. Academics may disparage it, but writing which foregrounds personality and subjectivity has implicitly at least the blessing – and encouragement – of editors. Even the most serious broadsheets have expanded their amount of first-person writing, recognising the pulling power of individuals and personalities. The websites created by conventional newspapers like the *New York Times*, the *Guardian* and the *Telegraph* have heavily invested in commentary with more visible, transparent subjectivity, where readers can interact with previously remote journalistic figures.

However, this should not imply that everything is rosy in first-person journalism. The preoccupation with witnessing intimate personal details combined with the tendency towards ever more extreme experiences has consequences both for the ordinary people whose stories are told and for journalists. Journalism's appetite for personal stories means ordinary people are at risk of exploitation because their reactions and feelings have become interesting to the public, particularly at times of distress. This happened to the McCann family after the abduction of Madeleine and the Dowler family after their daughter Millie was murdered. These families were subjected not only to critical commentary but had their private lives invaded by journalists looking to report on what the families were feeling. Thanks to investigative journalists at *Private Eye* and the *Guardian*, we know now just how far certain journalists were prepared to go in their search for intimate details, failing to observe either the law or basic decency.

For journalists who use their own lives as material, there are also risks – of alienating their friends and family, or finding themselves the subject of a hate campaign (and easily traceable via the Internet) for 'exploiting real people'. There are the dilemmas of how to relate to readers when sharing details of broken relationships and terminal illnesses. Increasingly there are issues connected with the psychological motivation of journalists who make a living out of personal exposure, especially in the context of an increasing appetite for extreme experiences. There is a world of difference between Joan Didion's account of mourning and the *Daily Mail*'s confessional columnist Liz Jones describing stealing sperm from her ex-husband (*The Daily Mail* 3 November 2011). There are no road maps for journalists undertaking this kind of writing, nor is there any critical discourse to help editors and critics differentiate between journalism which has a genuinely useful social element and that motivated by exhibitionism.

These are pressing critical and ethical reasons for studying first-person journalism, but there are also literary critical reasons. Although first-person journalism appears as if coming unmediated from the heart, it is, just like any other kind of writing, built on conventions. Bizarrely, those most critical of this kind of journalism for triviality and dumbing down rarely question it as a literary construction. Instead, personal writing is treated as if it is 'the truth', autobiographical truth. Yet, no less than other writing, autobiographical writing adopts conventions, uses tropes and forms to gain attention and also to avoid some of those ethical dilemmas. Different kinds of personal writing are genres like any other: they have histories and roles, use established conventions and involve journalistic motivations. No one would dream of teaching a course about news which didn't include history, structures and conventions and often also the philosophical and reflexive issues that arise in these forms of writing. You wouldn't expect someone to enter into journalism without knowing this.

Yet for first-person writing – perhaps the biggest growth area of journalism – there is nothing. Insofar as there has been any critical attention to the formal issues of this kind of writing, it has been under the headings 'features' or in America, 'literary journalism'. So this book aims to fill the gaps. It will look at the history of personal journalism and particularly how journalism which speaks more personally has always been present (Chapter 1). It will look at the areas of conventional journalism where a more personal voice has always been present and follow how this has become more audible (Chapter 2). It will look at the journalism which foregrounded the personal voice and explore why (Chapters 3 and 4). And it will examine the dominant contemporary genres of personal writing (Chapters 5, 6, and 7), their conventions and their ethical issues.

1 The Impersonal Voice and the Fallacies of Objectivity

Ideals of objectivity and impartiality are among journalism's most deeply cherished and hard-won ideals, and are generally seen as threatened by the recent explosion of more subjective 'authored' forms of writing like columns and blogging. 'Objectivity' and 'impartiality' usually assume the journalist is a detached observer whose subjectivity is invisible and irrelevant. Yet the 'authorial voice' – a distinctive voice with a subjectivity and personal address – is not a new phenomenon in the history of journalism. The following chapter looks at how authorial, subjective voices have long been present in editorials, opinion pieces, advocacy and classic reportage, often playing a crucial role in engaging readers and sometime helping reinforce beliefs in objectivity. This type of journalism is rarely given prominence or value in journalism studies, but has produced some of the greatest, most enduring, pieces of journalism.

What is objective journalism?

Critical writing on journalism long ago suggested that the idea of a neutral observer who transparently reports on facts without having a position on them, or affecting them, by his or her presence is problematic. Like other branches of social sciences, journalism studies recognised that so-called scientific objectivity is inevitably a position or an attitude towards its material so embedded it is no longer visible. Yet the ideal remains potent in journalism. Critics might acknowledge the concept's limitations, but it is still the default ideal surfacing in laments over declining journalistic standards and anxieties about journalism's future.

Franklin, talking about how proper news has gone down market and become 'newszak' implicates the replacement of facts by opinions: 'the commentariat are in the ascendency' (2008, p. 14). British journalism, says Harding (2011, p. 32), is at 'risk going down the same route as the United States. We will end up with a whole string of strident Fox News- and MSNBC-style channels.' For many critics, the Internet is the apotheosis of these negative trends, a babbling mass where strident subjectivity and personal opinion hold sway. 'A universe that was once well-ordered, well-mannered and well-balanced in its arguments is now fragmented, diverse, complex, messy, shouting', says Marsh, characterising those fears. 'Every possible view of the world is expressed somewhere, and new ones are being invented all the time. And why shouldn't anyone be free to choose only those accounts of the world that confirm their prejudices?' (*Press Gazette* 29 July 2007).

Behind these comments lies the notion that subjectivity, personal opinion and partisan commentary are the enemies of good journalism. Ron Rosenbaum, journalist and sometime professor at Columbia Journalism School, argues this assumption still predominates in many journalism schools. The subjective voice is disparaged compared with what is regarded as 'proper' journalism – news and reportage. 'The term "straight reporting" carries an assumption of superiority', he says, adding that 'the atmosphere of J-schools is dominated by those who sneer at anything but voiceless journalism – a sneer that is confusing to students and is, alas, based on philosophic fallacies' (*The New York Observer* 26 August 2002). In UK journalism schools, proper journalism is 'hard news' – accurate, impersonal and objective – while personalised or subjective writing is cast as soft and unreliable.

This notion of objective journalism is 'a late comer to journalism' (Marsh 2007), an ideal which only coalesced into a discernible style of writing and professional ideology in the early decades of the twentieth century. This evolution has been well documented especially in America where, 'If American journalism were a religion...its supreme deity would be objectivity' (Mindich 1998, p. 1). But on both sides of the Atlantic devotion to impartial facts, presented in a particular style, slowly nudged aside the 'ragged and confusing' jumble of different styles and voices which was the 'prehistory of modern journalism' (Marr 2005, p. 6). Reportage of the kind which evolved into what we recognise as modern journalism did exist: Marr describes Daniel Defoe as having 'created a journalistic style that lasted' and attributed this to a combination of clear succinct writing and a commitment to 'proper reporting' (Marr 2005, p. 8). But numerous other styles existed too, including political essays, artisan pamphlets and scandal sheets.

Much early journalism was openly partisan: the high level of stamp duty on newspapers effectively prevented publication of anything not subsidised by political parties or campaigns. Consequently, dominant writing styles were openly partial and authorial, like that of the

Economist, launched in 1843 to campaign for free trade and against the Corn Laws. It was only in June 1855, with the removal of the final penny of stamp duty, that British newspapers became commercially viable. This produced an explosion in newsprint seeing the establishment of not just serious papers like the *Telegraph* and the *Times* but also new, more popular, forms of journalism covering daily events and human interest stories aimed at mass audiences. Mass circulation transformed newspapers into valuable businesses, bringing in entrepreneurs like Beaverbrook and Northcliffe in Britain and Hearst and Pulitzer in the United States, who saw that owning a successful newspaper was a route not just to wealth but also influence.

While these proprietors often committed their newspapers to definite political postures, newspapers in general started to be seen less as vehicles for one person's or a party's opinions and more as providers of information. Even the more sensationalist and human interest newspapers were accompanied by an emerging taste for facts 'telling it as it is' over the sometimes-wild and outlandish stories which had dominated the penny press in the immediate aftermath of lifting the stamp duty (Marr 2005). Editions of the *Times* at the turn of the century illustrate how conventions associated with objective journalism emerged slowly and unevenly. The front pages were mainly classified adverts followed by shipping and ecclesiastical news; large sections were devoted to law court reports as well as lengthy parliamentary debates and detailed listings. The modern news hierarchy and demarcations between editorial styles and reportage were not consistently in place.

Unlike modern journalism, reports were often longer, more discursive and included subjective impressions and interpretations evident in the use of emotive adjectives. 'Two admirable speeches were made yesterday', wrote our 'own correspondent' under the headline, 'Italy's sacrifices. Appeal for further effort' (*The Times* 13 February 1918). Although a report from a correspondent, it is heavily editorialised. 'Italy will answer the appeal for effort and sacrifice. No one who with sympathy and understanding has lived through the difficulties and anxieties of the last three months here can doubt that she will answer. She has stood the test: she has given the proof' (*The Times* 13 February 1918). It is only as the twentieth century advances that classic devices of objective reportage emerge: the bald statement of fact, shaved of subjective interpretation and spoken impersonally.

Schudson's history of journalism in America describes how a number of factors converged to create this style. Among other things, it reflected a new respect with which facts were treated in the late nineteenth century, thanks to the rise of science and the development of realism in literature (Schudson 1978, Stephens 2006). In addition there was the development of the wire service emerging from the new technology of telegraphic communication around 1840. The wire revolutionised journalism because it allowed rapid communication of news. But it was expensive, so newspapers pooled together to form the Associated Press. This resulted in a form writing which avoided any stylistic embellishments offering only 'facts' in order to be useable by all parties.

The same factors were at play in Britain, where the arrival of telegraphy and the Associated Press probably only reinforced a development with other roots (Allan 2004). These included the emergence of urban mass society and the general artistic and cultural interest in realism which was already apparent in the commitment of newspapers like the *Times* to accuracy and the importance of facts above everything (Williams 1998). Whatever the causes, by the turn of the century, good journalism was regarded as 'writing which was impartial, stood back from the scenes, witnessed and reported on them confining itself entirely to the facts' (Allan 2004, p. 19).

Marr describes the four things the Victorians did 'which made Britain the newspaper mad nation it remains even today'. 'They cut the taxes and lifted the legal restraints which had stopped papers being profitable; they introduced machinery to produce them in large numbers; they educated a population to read them; and they developed the mass democracy which made them relevant' (Marr 2005, p. 13). Marr highlights the important association being forged between newspapers and democracy, slightly surprising given the commercial foundation of the press. Objectivity is 'a very peculiar demand to make of institutions which as business corporations, are dedicated first of all to economic survival. It is a peculiar demand to make of institutions which often by tradition or explicit credo are political organs. It is a peculiar demand to make of editors and reporters who have none of the professional apparatus which for doctors or lawyers or scientists is supposed to guarantee objectivity' (Schudson 1978, p. 3).

Yet, however commercial (indeed for some periods, wildly profitable), news organisations were increasingly recognised as having a key role in modern democracies allowing citizens to access accurate information. The job of reporters came to be seen as uncovering and recounting facts with impartiality not one of cheerleading for the particular political party supported by their newspaper. More and more, news was considered an independent substance, composed of facts; opinion as something else entirely, something slightly 'disreputable', according to

Stephens (2006). The more discursive story-based journalism and the more partisan or opinionated pieces began to be seen as lesser forms of journalism: Schudson describes how the *New York Times* came to be seen as a higher form of journalism than the more story-based *New York World*.

Miraldi describes the journalistic ideals which emerged as 'a fact-orientated, impartial perspective, independent of state power, of advertisers, and of any special interest, one that allowed competing versions of the "truth" to appear before a rational, choosing public. The press would supply the public – and the decision-making elites – with the knowledge needed to make public policy decisions' (Miraldi 1990, p. 13). The discursive norms, practices and strategies associated with objective reporting have come to be seen as synonymous with the practice of journalism, a move which tends to mean other journalistic styles, including those which pre-existed them, are not viewed as proper journalism at all (Chalaby 1998). The link between these discursive norms of objective journalism and 'proper' journalism is also implicit in the idea of journalism as 'the fourth estate', that is serious journalism which holds politics and business to account and provides public forums in which informed debate can take place (Hampton 2010). Consequently, the objectivity of the press and the professionalism of journalists came slowly to be recognised as crucial elements in a democracy.

What does objectivity entail?

Given the importance this ideal has assumed for creating informed citizens able to make meaningful decisions in a free society, it is easy to see why 'objectivity' became – and remains – such a powerful ideal both for practising and trainee journalists. Yet it is less easy to specify what objectivity in journalism exactly is. That depends on whom you ask, says Mindich. 'For some it is a vague point to strive for. For others it involves specific practices' (Mindich 1998, p. 1). Objectivity is not easily defined and never has been. This ideal is no more than 'a rough and ready consensus' (Gaber 2009, p. 41).

In fact, the abstract ideal of objectivity is frequently defined by the practices associated with it. At the forefront are the styles and stances of journalists and journalistic culture. Tuchman (1972), describing the 'strategic rituals' of the newsroom, includes a state of 'detachment' from the events (not having a stake in them), non-partisanship (not taking sides, not promoting the interests of one particular party or individual), facticity (verification of facts) and balance (fairness, if there is a conflict of interpretation allowing the views of each side). 'According to professional standards, as they are usually taught in journalism schools, an objective journalist is un-biased, neutral, impartial, detached, balanced, invisible' (Kitch 1999, p. 114).

Along with these stances and values, one particular journalistic writing convention predominates: 'the inverted pyramid', whereby the essential information is established quickly at the beginning of an article. Padding such as adjectives – which inevitably introduce an element of subjective interpretation – would be cut first when space is short. Journalists are required to move swiftly to what happened, where and to whom, to gather opposing views, but not have a position. Interpretation is eliminated, the reporter acting instead as a neutral conduit to the audience who can then form their own opinions.

Of particular interest here is that for some critics, the values of 'impartiality' and 'fairness' have become synonymous with a particular style of writing and one that requires a 'detached' journalistic voice. In Narrative Journalism comes of Age, Kramer describes the voice of a news reporter as rather like a police report. 'Its very "personalitylessness"', he says, 'makes the voice so handy – and thrifty'. Unlike personal styles reporters might use to describe the same fire to their friends down the pub, 'It can be imitated by any reporter ... and it can be deployed to good effect by writers of moderate verbal skill. It enables sending reporters where needed, like police officers sent to changeable beats.' News voice is 'intentionally bland, non-judgmental, quirk-free, and responsible and sober, a useful presence interested in names and affiliations and times and numbers' (Kramer 2000).

Kramer continues: 'If "style is personality", as the rhetorician Richard Lanham says, readers may detect little companionability in that persona. The news voice does not acknowledge the readers' savvy or know-how or sophisticated comprehension of motives, people, organizations or the world. It always starts explanations from scratch. Its job is to record, explain, to create a record, report – hardly to entertain.' Tellingly he adds 'herein lies its limitation: For all its civic utility, the news voice also limits the newspaper as good company for readers' (Kramer 2000).

These writing conventions can be easily learned, making them transferable between journalists. So as well as being socially important, fact-based, impartial and impersonal writing is practical. Yet there are many problems in the way this style of writing has come to be seen as the best, and sometimes the only, kind of journalism. Two problems are particularly significant: one is that objectivity is philosophically flawed and the other is that the values embodied in 'objectivity' – balance, accuracy, 'facticity' – are not synonymous with detachment and invisibility. Arguably the reverse is true, that greater transparency means greater accountability.

Philosophical fallacies of objectivity

Behind apparently neutral reports there's invariably an edifice of assumptions, as this *Daily Telegraph* (22 August 2011) report shows: 'The body of a 77-year-old spinster, Judith Richardson, was discovered at her home in Hexham, Northumberland, after her handbag was found in a bin 22 miles away. Mrs Richardson was bludgeoned to death in her flat in the Northumberland town, where she lived alone in what is thought to be a burglary. She was seen walking her highland terrier, Hamish, on Friday morning in the quiet country town where she lives.' A number of assumptions are in play. Firstly the murder is covered because it fulfils prevailing news values: it is a crime (sensationalist, interesting), but it's also a crime in a small, usually peaceful village (unexpected, out of the usual). A number of other values surreptitiously enter the statement. The victim is a 'spinster', not just elderly, but unmarried (therefore especially vulnerable and alone), her dog called 'Hamish' (local, stereotypically Scottish), she's in a 'quiet' town. In other words, this is especially vicious and unexpected – a juxtaposition of horror and timidity. This is a verifiable record of events but what looks neutral in fact positions readers into certain interpretations.

Even the most neutral 'objective' reports, stripped down to the bare facts, can actually be very slanted due to the framing of the report: what the newspaper has covered before, its news values and the juxtaposition of articles: 'A failed asylum seeker who committed 26 crimes within six years of arriving in the UK could win damages after a judge ruled that he had been unlawfully detained by immigration authorities' (*The Daily Mail* 26 August 2011). This passage technically meets the criterion of 'objective' writing being impersonal, neutral and an accurate record of a legal situation. But plenty would dispute its 'objectivity', occurring in the context of a newspaper with a number of related running preoccupations – the difficulty of removing failed asylum seekers, the apparent use of human rights legislation to protect criminals and the 'problem' of immigration of the 'wrong sort'. What appears a neutral sentence in fact positions the reader into sharing certain assumptions.

The principle extends into weightier subjects. News values, the implicit position and the sources all frame what information is selected and how it is presented. Coverage of the Iraq War in March 2003 has been widely discussed as an area where many branches of the media failed to question the war's legality accepting the claims made in various government dossiers justifying invasion. Chomsky (2003) has pointed out how US coverage was triumphalist, neglected negative effects of the allied invasion and took as its starting point the government position. Journalism here not only failed to be 'neutral' but also potentially influenced events. The 'journalistic belief in objectivity', writes Gaber, is based on one of the great 'truths of journalism which is in fact a great lie' (Gaber 2009, p. 41).

'Objectivity' assumes detachment from the world that is unattainable; no one is able to detach their emotions, their fundamental beliefs and their world view from every situation creating themselves as a sort of tabula rasa. Neither is 'neutrality' a genuine possibility. That means never making a judgement, yet judgements are constantly made about who to interview (sources), what to show and what is considered the most important fact. 'Impartiality often means making real-world judgements – such as weighing a mainstream against a minority one' (Marsh 2007). The stance implicit in 'neutrality' is based on selectivity – about the subjects deemed worth covering, and about the people who are deemed fit to cover them: 'two aspects are at the heart of debate about journalistic and historical objectivity: what subject matter is considered professional and what role the researcher/reporter plays in how those subjects are researched and written about' (Kitch 1999, p. 116).

There have been many challenges to this position, but one of the clearest examples came from the challenge of women's representation in the journalism. 'Representation' here means both how women are represented in the journalistic text and how they are represented in the journalistic workforce. In the 1970s, women argued that not only were they under-represented in newspapers, but also there was wider discrimination in journalistic content and how issues were covered. Women journalists had often found themselves confined to covering 'feminine' subjects which had low status and often not even considered newsworthy.

With the emergence of feminism, it was realised that these marginal, so-called female issues were ones which affected women's opportunities. They were in fact important subjects, newsworthy certainly to those affected by them, but rendered less important by the news hierarchy. Those who wrote about them were considered less serious journalists.

Women challenged not only these news values but some of them also challenged the dominant style, embracing more subjective modes of address and drawing inspiration from the feminist slogan of the era, 'the personal is political'. This will be explored in Chapter 4 but for now it illustrates how objectivity claimed by journalism can be highly ideological – an edifice built on a hierarchy of news values, embedded perspectives and voices which, although supposed to be neutral, represent certain values.

Objectivity and reportage

The journalistic ideal of objectivity is not only a philosophical fallacy, but it is also built on a paradox. On the one hand, conventions of objectivity require that reporters distance themselves from the scene, reporting as if invisible. On the other, reportage – the cornerstone of journalism – is premised on the first-person presence of the observer. In fact, the greatest and most enduring pieces of journalism are often those where the observer has been recognisable as a personality either through their individual style or through foregrounding their presence including very often their own reactions to events. 'There are consistent departures', says Kitch, 'from our detachment ideals and ironically some of these departures are among the most celebrated form of journalism' (Kitch 1999, p. 117).

Journalism's professional conventions may have ossified into an impersonal style for reporting news, but reportage with a stronger authorial presence has always flourished. Those who brought more of themselves as authors into situations they witnessed often created the most vivid and lasting reports. Arguably this writing endures not in spite of, but precisely because, along with the events' description, came a sense of the writers and their reactions. Embodying this paradox is the fact that 'finding your own voice' as a reporter remains one of the highest aspirations of today's journalism students, encouraged even in those very journalism schools which heap opprobrium on personal writing.

As already described, the rigid stylistic conventions of objective reporting only came to dominate around the time of the First World War. Prior to that early journalism, although often unattributed, or presented under pseudonyms, was far more discursive and subjective, full of first-hand accounts. Much nineteenth-century journalism is based on this unspoken contract between reader and writer, that the 'I' will tell the truth. Like early travel writing with accounts of distant lands, 'truthfulness' was established by the eye witness. In the days before visual recording, or instant transmission, there had to be trust that reporters will tell what he or she has really seen. 'You can believe it because I was there; I witnessed this with my own eyes' is a cornerstone of journalism and remained at the heart of journalistic conventions even as they consolidated at the end of the nineteenth century.

Before the establishment of rigid writing conventions, writers un-self-consciously wrote themselves into the picture. Writing in Dickens' magazine, *Household Words* in 1856 for example, Eyre Crowe, a British artist who accompanied Thackeray to America, was typical of the period in, including his 'first hand observation' of a slave auction, describing how the traders suspected his presence, and how he was 'followed suspiciously' especially 'if carrying a pencil'. What he saw appalled him too and he made his politics explicit, concluding with a passionate call for the abolition of slavery. Many of the most memorable and enduring pieces of reportage of the nineteenth century were, like Crowe's, not only vivid eyewitness accounts but also discursive, personal and opinionated. Henry Mayhew was a Victorian social reformer and journalist whose *London Labour and the London Poor* is regarded as one of the most valuable, detailed and accurate pictures of poverty in this period. Mayhew's descriptions are based on immersion of himself in the situation, exhaustive questioning of his subjects and faithful reproduction of dialogue. These techniques – immersion, interviewing, and dialogue- are the techniques of classic reportage. Along with forensic interest in the lives and occupations of the poor, his writing is also scenic and discursive and makes no attempt to hide its author. Indeed Mayhew often foregrounds how he conducted his research; in one typical sequence, he harries a costermongers' girl who is reluctant to be interviewed. Mayhew's personality shows through not just because of the inclusion of himself but also his idiosyncratic interests, individualistic observations and strong 'moral' voice. After witnessing what he considered a particularly 'debased' display by some of the costermongers' lads he writes, 'My own experience with this neglected class goes to prove that if we would really lift them out of the moral mire in which they are wallowing the first steps must provide them with some wholesome amusement' (Mayhew 1861, 2011 edition, p. 42).

Randall's *The Great Reporters* (2005) includes several writers whose passions, perceptions and responses were likewise at the forefront of their journalism, leading them not to impartiality but to taking sides. One of them, William Howard Russell, a friend of Dickens and other leading intellectuals of the day, wrote for the *Times*, from 1845 onwards covering major events including the Crimean War. He was scrupulous in detailing what he saw, as well as collecting first-hand accounts, but he is still celebrated for his vivid personal style, his evocative description and clear judgements. 'I shall precede to describe' opens his devastating account of the Charge of the Light Brigade, 'to the best of my power what occurred under my own eyes and to state the facts which I have heard from men whose veracity is unimpeachable, reserving to myself... the right of private judgement in making public and superseding the details of what occurred on this memorable day' (Russell 1854, p. 333). What follows is legendary both for its evocation of the beauty of the surroundings which contrasted so painfully with the battle's horror and also for its devastating exposé of the mistakes which led to the slaughter.

Russell was nothing if not partisan. When he witnessed first-hand British atrocities in India, he became an outspoken critic of the racism of the system: 'That force is the base of our rule I have no doubt; for I see nothing else but force employed in our relations with the governed. The grave unhappy doubt which settles on my mind is whether India is better for our rule' (Russell 1858, p. 2). His vacillating views also led to him offending both sides in the American Civil War.

Reporters were not just visible through their opinions but through personal style too: Russell's attention to his surroundings, the weather and the sword flashes of the Light Brigade is almost poetic. Some of the greatest pieces of journalism have come from the greatest stylists – novelists, or at least writers who moved between fiction and non-fiction imprinting their distinctive personality, viewpoint and social or political values on their writing. In America, Mark Twain and Jack London were both great reporters as well as great novelists. Twain's piece 'My Debut as a Literary Person' (Twain reprinted 1995), an account of how his journalistic career was kick-started when a great story fell into his lap, would make illuminating reading for contemporary journalism students about the rewards for persistence and recognising the significance of what is under your own nose.

In England, Dickens started his career as a journalist, first as a parliamentary reporter where his brilliance at capturing and conveying scenes was soon recognised (Tomalin 2011), then moving on to write 'sketches' of people and places. His first paid work was the commission of magazine pieces printed together as *Sketches by Boz* in 1836. Even after the huge success of his first novel, *Pickwick Papers*, journalism remained important to him. It's estimated he wrote over a million words over his lifetime (Tulloch 2007) and throughout his career he was constantly founding magazines and outlets for his and others' journalism, never exhibiting any snobbery towards journalism as an inferior form to fiction.

Dickens' journalism was more than stylised: it was rhetorical. Addressing his 'dear reader', his journalistic alter ego, Boz, was partial, partisan and passionate, a campaigner who saw journalism's potential as a weapon of social reform. His writing was invariably subjective with himself as author in the foreground. In 'Night walks' (July 1860), Dickens paces around London at night, observing in great detail the people of the night – the homeless, the scavengers – the side of London his middle-class contemporaries never saw. But the piece starts with an account of the insomnia that drives him to the streets and quickly establishes his empathy – bordering on identification – for the restless people of the night. The writing is not only personal but also self-referential, betraying much about Dickens himself (Tulloch 2007). Yet it's no less a powerful account of the streets of London for that.

Bagehot despised Dickens for his rhetoric, his caricatures and his sentimentality. Nevertheless he paid tribute to Dickens for his eyewitness accounts, the vividness with which he recorded scenes and his ear for dialogue saying Dickens had described London like a 'special correspondent for posterity' (Bagehot 1858). It's an interesting comment because it acknowledges how in spite of the very obvious presence of Dickens in the forefront of everything he writes, either directly as an 'I' or indirectly through his distinctive style, he is still providing an authentic and lasting report about London.

Kerrane and Yagoda pay tribute to his reportage when including Dickens' piece, 'The Great Tasmanian Cargo', in their collection, the *Art of Fact*, a selection of journalism which they claim transcends the mundane and becomes art (Kerrane and Yagoda 1998). This is classic Dickens, an attack on the mistreatment of soldiers, who, shipped back to England after a supposed mutiny, arrived in the most shocking state. The piece includes 'composite characters', that is figures, made up of various parts of a number of different 'typical' characters rather than a real individual. In this case, the figure is a representative of the Circumlocution Office, a character which is used later in his novel, *Little Dorrit*, to embody obfuscating bureaucracy. Composite characters became and remain anathema to 'objective' journalism. Nevertheless Kerrane and Yagoda point out this article has key journalistic strengths: the power of description, the author's indignation and one classic piece of 'interlocution of the good sergeant' which they say could be used as 'a model in a journalism school of interviewing'. Admittedly Dickens was already a celebrity at this point and using his fame. But the subjective presence he deploys by no means gets in the way of the reportage. He interacts with the protagonists, participates in scenes and seethes with indignation at the prisoners' treatment and the hypocrisy of officialdom. Many of these elements – the hyperbole, the rhetorical flights, the composite characters – came to be regarded as unacceptable in 'proper' reportage. Nevertheless as with so much of Dickens' journalism, the piece remains as vivid as if written today.

Dickens was not unique. Many of the journalists of the time – certainly those whose work has been preserved – wrote in this more partisan and self-referential way. George Augustus Sala was spotted by Dickens, who published his first work in his magazine *Household Words*. Sala's career took off and he became one of the best known and influential journalists of the era, writing regularly for the *Daily Telegraph* shortly after its launch in the mid-1800s. Sala's style was distinctive to the point of overblown. Writing on one of London's shopping arcades, he typically proclaimed: 'But the arcade is so dull. Some ghastly artist undertook, on its construction, to decorate it with mural arabesques. He has succeeded in filling the spaces between the shop-windows with some skeleton figures; – dripping, faded funerealities' (Sala 1859, p. 192). Much of Sala's work was also highly self-referential with his larger-than-life character at the forefront. 'I have no bed tonight', he writes melodramatically at the start of *Gaslight and Daylights*: 'Why it matters not. Perhaps I have lost my latch key – perhaps I never had one, yet I am fearful of knocking up my landlady after midnight. Perhaps I have a caprice – a fancy – for stopping out all night. At all events I have no bed and saving sixpence, no money' (Sala 1859, p. 1). In a 2007 catalogue produced by London's National Portrait Gallery catalogue, it was said he 'wrote about every issue of the day in an exuberant, often amusing manner but whatever the ostensible subject matter, he mostly wrote about himself'. Yet like Dickens this personalised, distinctive opinionated writing did not detract from vivid and lasting reportage.

Sala had a remarkable career as a journalist. As the *Daily Telegraph*'s foreign correspondent, his own sympathies and views were so prominent that he became extremely unpopular for his reports on the American Civil War (where he sympathised with the South). He also became a prolific leader writer. His writing was often parodied, for its bombastic, egotistical, hyperbolic tendencies and became the butt of jokes about the *Telegraph*'s style. But he exercised considerable influence, partly on public opinion as a direct result of his trenchant, campaigning journalism (sometimes even on progressive causes) and partly on the direction of journalism itself. He created a place for popular journalistic campaigning and is attributed with being the major influence on WT Stead, editor of the *Pall Mall Gazette* and *Illustrated London News*. Stead is now best known perhaps for his untimely – and apparently predicted – death on the Titanic but as another trenchant writer, who investigated among other things the exploitation of underage girls, is regarded as a pioneer of the popular campaigning style now known as tabloid journalism.

As can be seen, many of these were writers who crossed the line from reporting into campaigning or reform (as they called it in Britain) or advocacy (in America). Randall also includes in his collection work by Nellie Bly, who was described at her death by the United States' leading editor, Arthur Brisbane, as 'quite simply the best reporter who ever lived'. Much of her writing is highly personalised, ranging from the frivolous – if nevertheless bold – undertaking of her version of Verne's journey round the world, serialised by Pulitzer in the *New York World* between 1889 and 1890, to serious undercover reporting on mental asylums. Her piece, 'Inside the Madhouse', written in 1887 (Belford 1986) is often held up as one of the great pieces of investigative reporting and has many similarities with contemporary first-person pieces, especially the foregrounding of her own subterfuge. Randall also includes work by Ida Tarbell, who wrote an extended piece of journalism for McClure's about the activities of Standard Oil Company under the control of Roosevelt, exposing the company's monopolistic practices and strong arm tactics. Tarbell was a scrupulous reporter who crossed the line from dispassionately recording facts to a commitment to exposing a wrong. Americans gave the term 'muckraking' to her writing, a term she disliked, but her text is still regarded as a founding piece of investigative journalism. 'The point of view of the muckraker – an adversarial, critical, outsider's point of view – is far afield from the one that dominates the conventional press, that is, the objective or neutral point of view. The objective journalist is simply an observer who follows events, describes occurrences, provides background, and perhaps lends perspective, but he or she is not an active partner in shaping events or reforming society. The journalist is a neutral technician who, in the end, is an unknowing partner in shaping events and reforming society. The activist tradition of muckraking collides head on with objectivity, this fetish of the mainstream press' (Miraldi 1990, p. 17).

It could be argued that all these writers were simply products of their time, their writing infused by the stylistic traits of the period – more discursive, more opinionated, more directly personal and in some cases like Dickens and Twain operating on the margins between literature and journalism. But even when news writing conventions were fully established, there continued to be reporters who brought themselves into the picture with huge effect. This is the case of many of the great journalists of the twentieth century, such as George Orwell, whose powerful accounts of the Spanish Civil War came from the front line not as a detached observer but as a participant. After being hit by a bullet for example, he wrote of the experience as being 'very interesting...and I think worth describing in detail'. 'Roughly speaking it was like being in the centre of an explosion. There was a loud bang and a blinding light all around me, and I felt tremendous shock – no pain, only a violent shock, such as you get from an electric terminal; with it an utter sense of weakness, a feeling of being stricken and shrivelled up to nothing. The sandbags in front of me receded into immense distance. I fancy you would feel much the same if you were struck by lightning. I knew immediately I was hit' (Orwell 1937, p. 521).

This war produced a number of great reporters, who sent back vivid eyewitness accounts that also detailed their reactions to the events they witnessed. Martha Gellhorn and James Cameron are viewed as great reporters whose passions and commitments were often visible. Martha Gellhorn, like Orwell, was passionately engaged by the Spanish Civil War and the threat of fascism, and her left wing, anti-fascist politics were always near the surface in her reports. After visiting a hospital in Spain in 1937, Gellhorn said she was not concerned with reporting objectively, 'You go into a hospital and it's full of wounded kids. So you write about what you see. You don't say there are 37 wounded children in this hospital, but maybe there are 38 on the other side. You write about what you see' (cited in MacLoughlin 2007, p. 65). Indeed, she considered the ideal of journalistic objectivity 'nonsense'.

Gellhorn's account of entering Dachau concentration camp is widely regarded as one of the most devastating reports of the Second World War. She was with troops when they went into the camp in May 1945 and her report is as shocking today as then. Again, there is no attempt at journalistic invisibility. She describes not only the sight of the starving survivors, but also her reaction. When one Polish doctor describes the experiments carried out on camp inmates, Gellhorn recounts, 'we did not look at each other. I do not know how to explain it but aside from the terrible anger, you feel you are ashamed. You are ashamed for mankind.' 'Then', she continues, 'because I could listen no more, my guide, a German socialist who had been in prison for 10 and half years took me across the compound to the jail. In Dachau, if you want to rest from one horror you go and see another.' Viewing the bodies, she reflects on the role of the reporter and foregrounds her feelings: 'we have all seen a great deal now, we have seen too many wars and too much violent dying; we have seen hospitals, bloody and messy as butcher shops; we have seen the dead like bundles lying on the roads of half the earth. But nowhere was there anything like this. Nothing about war was ever as insanely wicked as these staved and outraged, naked and nameless dead' (MacLoughlin 2007, p. 17). Bill Buford, literary editor of *The New Yorker*, said it was her eloquent outrage which made her such an exceptional reporter. Far from the detached observer, what makes her reports so potent is that she recorded and included her human reactions.

British journalist and war correspondent James Cameron was not as outspoken in his political views, but he also frequently made his own reactions and commitments visible. Like Gellhorn, he is often held up as an exemplary reporter, but he too was passionate, individualistic and engaged. The impact of Cameron's writing was heightened by his eloquent style and apposite phrasing, which seemed to bring to life whatever he was describing, whether it was his own trade: 'the inky, edgy, clatter some and voracious occupation that was well called the press' (Cameron 1984), or the horrendous conditions of Korean prisoners of war: 'They have been in jail now for indeterminate periods – long enough to have reduced their frames to skeletons, their sinews to string, their faces to a translucent terrible grey, their spirit to that of cringing dogs' (*Picture Post* 7 October 1950). But he also openly admitted his own viewpoint. On one occasion he described himself as a moderately indifferent reporter, describing how he couldn't cover things when he didn't care about them: 'I was never interested in writing about things in which I didn't feel at least moderately engaged' (Cameron 1984).

In 1950, *Picture Post* sent Cameron and photographer Bert Harding to Korea, where they discovered atrocities committed by the West's allies, South Korea, against the North Koreans. They stumbled upon what amounted to a concentration camp, with prisoners who had been there for years, starving. In fact his article was never published because of its sensitivity, but, talking about how he did everything to guarantee its publication, Cameron gives telling insight into his journalistic values. 'I drove it as far as I could. I wrote and re-wrote it until the article was almost austere. I didn't want people to think it was James Cameron being emotional. I never worked so hard to write so badly' (Cameron 1984). Cameron's reputation was for his reportage, yet, in his own eyes, unless he involved himself and his emotions, he thought he was writing badly. Cameron's prose usually emanated a strong commitment to his subject and conveyed a tangible personality which not surprisingly made an easy transfer to television where Cameron later became a familiar figure.

Cameron could perhaps be taken as the model for the most highly regarded contemporary journalists. Writers like John Pilger and John Simpson put themselves and their personalities very much in the foreground. Pilger makes no apology for writing committed journalism where his own politics are there for everyone to see. But even Simpson, whose journalism is more in the tradition of objective reporting, is no less inclined to let his larger-than-life personality and views be seen occasionally, to the extent that on one occasion he was extensively teased for his account of the liberation of Kabul. 'His suggestion on the Today programme', said the *Guardian* (19 November 2001), 'that "it was only BBC people who liberated this city – we got in ahead of Northern Alliance troops" provoked hilarity and ridicule from broadcasting rivals'. Simpson was forced to say he regretted 'getting a bit carried away'.

Conclusion

Are these writers any less objective? Are they any less accurate? Does the fact that we know what they think and feel about the scenes they are witnessing undermine information they have to convey? The answer is an emphatic 'no'. Accurate reportage, bearing witness by presence, recording what you have seen is not compromised by the admission of subjective presence and personal reactions. James Fenton, writing in the 1970s, went to the heart of the matter, arguing that reportage, where the journalist witnessed with their own eyes and was visible to the reader, was the fundamental activity of journalism. 'By reporting I mean something that predates journalism – the fundamental activity.' He continued 'journalism becomes quite unnatural when it strays too far from its origins. It is quite astonishing to me how much interesting material is jettisoned by newspaper reporters because they know they will not be able to write it up because to do so would imply they had been present at the events they are describing. And not only present – alive, conscious and with a point of view' (Fenton 1988 cited Kerrane and Yagoda 1998).

What makes reportage enduring, readable across the gulf of time is often that we can see and hear the reporters themselves as feeling, thinking, human beings. This is *why* they are great writers and why such writing is particularly powerful in forums of war: what actually conveys the true horror is not impartial description but how it affects the person who observes it. Arguably that is a more truthful account than a record of events delivered by a detached individual.

Yet this position is not without problems, foremost of which is the danger that the human and personal reactions become the story rather than what the journalist is ostensibly reporting on. This chapter has shown this is not a new phenomenon – indeed Bagehot's objections to Dickens might be seen as objections to a journalism where the writer's distinctive style and preoccupations are so much in the foreground they overwhelm the subject. The same doubt has been raised about Stead's campaigning on young prostitutes (Robinson 2012). Was this as much about his own preoccupations as the girls he campaigned for?

Fears that the subjectivity of the reporter is becoming too prominent have escalated from the 1960s onwards where, especially under the influence of television, the presence of reporters and their reactions has become ever more visible. Some critics (Wright 2012) have suggested that reporters like Michael Buerk and Fergal Keene might overwhelm situations with their own emotive reactions and agendas. Instead of an understanding of the wider social and cultural background of the issues, the Ethiopian famine became more about the pain of the observer. However, this may result from the nature of television as a journalistic medium. As Ellis, Peters and others (Frosh and Pinchevski 2009) point out, television allows viewers to 'see events for themselves', and also to judge the truthfulness of the reporter from their body language. This inevitably tips a TV report towards the emotional, and the power of these reports lies in part in seeing that reporters themselves cannot help but express their feelings. On the other hand, film is always specific, showing a particular place and time. The TV news reporter always has to work with the footage they managed to shoot. Newspaper journalists do not suffer from this constraint, able to generalise, to summarise and to analyse; in short to move smoothly from one register of writing to another.

Another considerable risk is that while the inclusion of the individual and the position from which they are talking might allow for more transparency, the individual may not be deserving of our trust. The responses foregrounded might be lies, dubious reactions and deliberate manipulation. They might be promoted by organisations with a vested interest in an outcome rather than a commitment to fact checking or accuracy.

Both these worries remind us of the importance of the professional values which surround the reporter and return us to objective journalism's fundamental values. This chapter has cast doubt on reportage delivered from a detached stance or by an apparently absent personality but not on the *values* embedded in the notion of objectivity. These values – of accuracy, fairness and facticity – evolved under the influence of an idea that journalism should serve the public interest in its broadest sense. And as organisational values and professional aspirations, they remain of inestimable importance in anchoring reportage as reliable, truthful and fair. From this perspective, the issue is not about subjectivity as the sui generis of reportage but as a transparent and necessarily human response set in a wider professional environment.

'As educators we should be teaching our students to be aware of their positions and how that affects what they report on, how they report it, and who gets a voice in its coverage', says Marsh (2007), an astute commentator: 'They may choose different positions depending on the nature of the subject, the medium, and the audience – playing to strengths rather than operating through habit. But if we see objectivity as just a badge to wear to make us different from our readers then we mistake the ends for the means. Objectivity is not setting down a convenient fence and selecting the people on either side that are easiest to reach – it is aspiring to create something that is representative of reality, while acknowledging and addressing the weaknesses in how we do that. And that includes being transparent.'

2 Changing Places: Opinion Columns and Editorials

More personal voices have long been present right at the heart of so-called objective journalism, namely in editorial and comment writing. Even in traditional quality newspapers, these forms are highly valued even though they depart from news writing conventions. Paradoxically these 'subjective' forms of writing are seen – when in the right place – as vital to journalism's claims to objectivity. The phrase 'in the right place' however signals ambivalence towards this kind of writing. Since the 1960s, commentary – particularly columns by named individuals – has steadily expanded. Since the 1980s, it has expanded exponentially, spilling out from designated comment sections. When sages bemoan the dumbed-down state of contemporary journalism, they invariably have in mind this post-1980s development. 'Once upon a time, both opinion writers and news journalists were easily recognizable by the public', laments Nord (2006). 'Political affiliations of newspapers were openly declared and could explain editorial positions on current events. Today by contrast news and views no longer seem to be in opposition to each other.'

This quote embodies widely held regret that the clear blue water which used to exist between commentary and news has been muddied, not just by tabloids where comment now occurs throughout the newspaper but by broadsheets themselves. In fact 'this right place' for commentary was late on the scene. Indeed it was only in the 1970s and 1980s that the classic op-ed format, whose passing is lamented in this quote, was widely adopted. The story of this section's evolution and of the changing relation between editorial, commentary and other journalism is an important one. It is not a story of inferior forms of journalism swamping the rest but of the steadily increasing importance of interpretation and subjective opinion.

The editorial voice and the op-ed voice

When commentators talk about the 'right place' for commentary, they have in mind today's classical broadsheet op-ed section. Typically a broadsheet op-ed section, like those in the *Times* and *Guardian*, contains three short editorials (or leaders), several comment pieces, readers' letters and, recently, editorial corrections and clarifications. In this design, editorials and commentary are segregated from the news not just in a separate section but employing different writing styles too.

Whereas news writing attempts to present facts without interference, leaving the reader to draw inference or make up their own mind, editorials by contrast have a clear point of view. They also have a personal voice although it is rarely synonymous with a real person such as the editor or owner. In the classic broadsheet model, editorials (leaders) are usually provided by specialist journalists or freelancers with relevant specialisms who adopt an opinionated but distant voice. In a recent *New York Times* editorial (19 October 2010), for example, the Iraqi prime minister's visit to neighbouring state is described as another 'international road trip' at a time when 'seven long months after parliamentary elections, Iraqis still don't have a government'. Mr Maliki is described as 'soliciting' neighbours' support when he should be building 'a legitimate government'. 'Meanwhile, almost nothing is happening in Iraq.'

Editorials use opinionated, interpretive, critical and emotive language; in this case encouraging readers to despise Maliki's actions as well as fearing the consequences of them. 'We were chilled by a report...that in recent months hundreds (or more) former Sunni fighters...have re-joined Al Qaeda.' There appears to be a personality behind the words, but it is not a colourful one. Instead it is lofty, authoritative and directive. 'Rather than trading unseemly favors [*sic*] with other countries, Mr Maliki should be working full time...to break the political impasse at home. Mr Allawi needs to be open to compromise.'

News reports would have simply informed the reader that Maliki was visiting neighbouring states, but this editorial interprets actions and motives, casting judgement on them: Maliki is travelling around because he has the wrong priorities. The editorial concludes with advice and exhortations addressed not to Maliki but to the government in Washington 'Iraq urgently needs a new government.... Washington needs to press all sides, a lot harder, to make a deal'.

Tabloid editorials are more direct, punchier and quicker to the point: 'Raising the motorway speed limit to 80 mph is long overdue', reads the *Sun*'s editorial (30 September 2011). 'The truth is that many drivers and police patrols already treat 10 over the 70 limit as acceptable. Lower 20 mph zones outside schools and residential areas save lives. But allow 80 on a motorway sounds to us very sensible.' But the function is identical to the broadsheets, drawing readers into a preferred understanding and, in constructing them as 'we', calling on policymakers to act in certain ways. The voice of these editorials is the voice of someone addressing politicians and government: 'the editorial is intended as a political intervention and is often read as such by a government or party' (McNair 1995, p. 13). 'It is in editorials that newspapers speak both for and to their audience, creating a distinctive voice for the newspaper which is otherwise buried under the conventions of objective journalism' (Wahl-Jorgensen 2008, p. 70).

If the editorial voice is institutional, the column is individual. In broadsheets, opinion columns are usually on pages opposite the editorial, hence 'op-eds'. Characteristically there are a number of diverse pieces provided by writers from different backgrounds. Some are journalists, some experts and some politicians who, although sharing cultural and political references, don't necessarily share political opinions.

According to various commentators, editorials and opinion pieces taken as a whole are 'central to a newspaper's identity. They are the only place in the paper where journalists are authorised to express opinion, often guided by the political leanings of the newspaper' (Wahl-Jorgensen 2008, p. 70). This is where the newspaper's political leanings and affiliations become visible and where the press gives voice to, intervenes in and sometimes shapes, public opinion. According to Santo (1994, p. 94) 'the most precise barometer of a newspaper's position on social and political questions is assumed to reside on the editorial page – the heart and soul and conscience of the newspaper'. Separated off from the news and clearly demarcated, this place gives the newspaper's politics visibility. This is the reason why critics are so anxious about its erosion. By seeing the newspaper's political parameters and hearing individual voices within those parameters, the reader can simultaneously receive the rest of the news as objective fact, while subliminally understanding the newspaper has a position which does not interfere with facts.

A cursory glimpse at the contemporary press shows how precarious this classic model is. The function of comment is not just, as is usually suggested, to interpret and analyse the news (McNair 2008), but also to express an individual view which engages and provokes the reader. Opinion columns not only use personal pronouns and even personal anecdotes, they require them. This writing is all about communicating a distinctive personality both in content and style – the more distinctive, the better. But unlike editorials, comment columns are not necessarily the views of the newspaper. Indeed, comment pages often allow views to be expressed which are more extreme than the newspaper's official view. I was aware of this over the many years in which I wrote for the *Guardian*'s comment and analysis pages. There was never any pressure exerted by editors to support or promote a particular political line. Rather the opposite; some editors appreciated it if the views put forward challenged certain orthodoxies. Some commentators like McNair (2008), acknowledging the diversity of comment writers' views, nevertheless suggest that all the writers selected for comment pages are 'authoritative', that is leading journalists, politicians, or experts in their field. The selection of these authority figures he suggests expresses what issues and which people a newspaper considers important. However, as will be discussed later, along with authority and knowledge, diversity and disagreement may be more important than all these critics suggest. These latter qualities have become even more important in the new online environment.

Since the 1980s, tabloids have increasingly blurred lines between news and comment. The middle market newspaper, the *Daily Mail*, is in some ways typical. It often has a main comment piece (written sometimes by outsiders or experts with strong opinions) alongside its three brief leaders. Regular commentators like Richard Littlejohn have their own pages while columnists like Melanie Phillips have a regular slot. Features with strongly personal points of view are scattered throughout. Nor is this integration of comment into the news only found in the tabloids. Strongly opinionated features, first-person pieces and comment columns also now appear scattered throughout all broadsheets. These organisations have massively expanded their commentary sections online.

But nostalgia for clear boundaries between editorial and news is misplaced. Demarcation between editorials and news only evolved slowly over the twentieth century, a process very much connected to reinforcing the emergent professional ideology of fact-based reporting. 'The belief in objectivity is a faith in "facts", a distrust in "values", and a commitment to their segregation (from opinion)', says Schudson (1978, p. 6). The classic op-ed section as described above only emerged finally in the 1970s in America and the 1980s in Britain. And although widely adopted, it has been over-spilling its 'proper place' ever since. This 'commentary explosion' (McNair 2008, p. 112) is one of journalism's most significant stories. It is not a story of decline but of evolution reflecting changing needs and functions for journalism.

Changing places: Editorials versus columns

The editorial as we now understand it – a distinct article separated from news, expressing not an individual or party's view but a newspaper's view – only emerged in Victorian Britain associated particularly with the *Times*. The precursor of the *Times*, the *Daily Universal*, was founded in 1785 (it became *The Times* in 1788) with a 'loan' from a government which expected a degree of control in return. But the newspaper gradually turned its back on this subsidy, favouring instead independence made possible by commercial viability, something which became easier after the repeal of the stamp duty. Increasingly, this independence came to mean providing a news service with an emphasis on accuracy and fact-based reporting as discussed in Chapter 1. It also led to eventual separation between editorial and reportage.

Early notions of leading articles tended to refer to short paragraphs of the news which the newspaper considered the most important (Liddle 1999). Journalism, more widely (as discussed in the previous chapter), was still often sponsored by parties so that partisan and persuasive rhetoric was very much in evidence. There were longer, more discursive pieces of writing in these early newspapers which tended to be supplied by writers – often readers – published pseudonymously under names like Decius. These articles appeared irregularly and somewhat randomly in the newspapers. Nevertheless by 1820 the term 'leading article' was being used to denote the editorial genre which was becoming 'the most important, authoritative and characteristic mode of British journalism, a position it would hold powerfully through much of the nineteenth century and formally until well into the twentieth century' (Liddle 1999, p. 5).

'For many mid-Victorian readers', says Liddle, 'a newspaper was its leading articles' (1999, p. 5). The popular name given to the *Times* was the Thunderer, a nickname for what Matthew Arnold called the 'trenchant authoritative style' (Arnold 1871, p. 119) with which the *Times* railed on the issues of the day. Writers were either anonymous or used pseudonyms; their voice was that of the *Times*, a 'quasi-mythical author': 'the voice of mentorship, guidance, and instruction in a leading article was simultaneously authorised and anonymous' (Liddle 1999, p. 13). The political influence of the newspaper grew steadily throughout the nineteenth century and was so great by the time of the Crimean War that the prime minister could 'bemoan the vile tyranny of the Times over the conduct of public affairs' (cited in Greenslade 2004).

Anonymous they may have been but leader writers were hugely important. 'From Victorian times to the 1980's', says Marr (2005, p. 367), 'few jobs were so highly rated at least by the people doing them, as leader writers. Teams of cerebral men, almost always men, in front of coal fires taunting one another with obscure Latin and Greek quotations, translating Proust in their spare time... used the anonymous leader columns to pursue pet causes, from tariff reform to ulster unionism. They felt themselves to be the soul of the paper, the essence of the Times or the Guardian. They thundered. They pleaded from their secular pulpits. The newspaper editorials were an important place for the national conversation to take place, well before the Today Programme or Question Time'.

The use of Latin declined but leading articles with their 'quasi-mythical' authors were soon widely adopted. Owners of course used their papers to directly express their own views – often explicitly in editorials as well as in the slant of the news. Lord Beaverbrook, for example, owner of, among other newspapers, the *Daily Express*, used editorials to push his agenda, including supporting appeasement in the run up to the Second World War. But, even where proprietors came to newspaper ownership not just to make money but to exercise political influence, the adopted editorial voice was institutional rather than proprietorial.

At the turn of the twentieth century, the *Times* layout was still a jumble of news, discursive reportage and leaders, but by the First World War some segregation emerged between news and editorials, a process duplicated across most other contemporary papers. 'By the time a professionalised press was making such distinctions, opinions, whether in the form of signed or unsigned editorials, or letters to the editor, began to be separated off from information, both in the self-understanding of journalists and in the layout of the papers' (Wahl-Jorgensen 2008, p. 71). This separation coincided with the adoption of the impersonal fact-based impersonal style of new reporting. The segregation had 'the effect of reinforcing the "facticity" of the news by offering a contained subjective counterpoint' (ibid., p. 71). Even so the modern editorial section, occupying a fixed and regular place in the newspapers, was not in place until some years later.

There was one significant difference between early and current editorial sections. Early editorial sections have no personalised, individually authored, attributable opinion pieces. But there are hints of what is to come. In early newspapers, readers' letters had far greater importance and space than in modern newspapers, filling almost all of what we now call the editorial page. The *Times* was particularly well known for its letters. *Times'* readers were establishment figures – bishops, headmasters of public schools, government ministers. Their addresses (always given) were often the House of Lords or the House of Commons. Right up to the 1960s, this was a hugely influential forum and writers considered it a matter of pride to be published. The role of modern comment pages was carried by these letters; they were a place of expertise, authority and debate about issues of public concern. Subjectivity and personality were visible, and there was interaction between readers who asserted views, were challenged by others and followed 'threads' to use contemporary terminology.

Through readers' letters, a series of views wider than newspaper's own were articulated, making it more a place of public opinion than institutional position. As with commentary now, letters to the editor communicated a newspaper's brand identity reflecting who their readers were and their everyday preoccupations. Editors soon realised the importance of readers' letters for bringing in the opinions, views, expertise and solutions being discussed in the public sphere. Publishers and editors also recognised their commercial value: the more opinionated and interactive style of journalism won over readers (Wahl-Jorgensen 2008, p. 71) and many letter writers were recruited as regular writers. In the mid-1800s Captain Edward Sterling, who began submitting letters to the *Times* under the name of Velus, was recruited to the editorial staff and became one of their most famous leader writers. In America, too, editors recognised the popularity of these sections, seeking out argumentative letters. The editor of *Boston Weekly Rehearsal* in the 1830s actively encouraged writers to express opinions of a political nature and, by the late 1800s some newspapers were paying for these submissions. 'A lot of the early copy that bore the marks of column writing was in the form of letters' (Riley 1998, p. 2).

Many of these early 'letter writers' were women, like Fannie Fern, who appeared regularly in the *New York Ledger*. During the nineteenth and early twentieth centuries, letters to the editor acted as pseudo-columns; it was common to regularly run letters from readers who were especially eloquent, engaging or representative of a constituency of interest. One of the most famous early American journalists, Nelly Bly (Elizabeth Cochran) came up through this route. An indignant letter to the *Pittsburgh Dispatch* about the treatment of women led to her being invited onto the staff. Letter writing is interpretative, opinionated and interactive and when authored columns emerged they took on these functions of interlocutor, analyst, expert, advocate and provocateur. This is the mode of address and reader relation which has steadily come to dominate journalism, first in the form of the authored column and increasingly with Internet commentary and blogging. As the individual provocative voice has become more prominent, the lofty impersonal voice of the editorial has all but disappeared.

The rise of the column

Column writing is a subject ripe for further research. Although it has increased steadily and relentlessly, it is not well studied. Column writing 'has a fragmented and slim knowledge base' (Duff 2008, p. 231), especially in relation to British journalism, where the genre developed later. 'Mass Communications scholarship has largely ignored the op-ed pages', say Day and Golan (2005, p. 62) while Duff (ibid., p. 231) asserts there is 'no clear cut cannon of academic knowledge about political columns'. There are many reasons for this neglect. At the forefront is a suspicious snobbery which denigrates personal voices as inferior journalistic forms. But the neglect also reflects the jumble of different types of writing, all known as columns, in other words a problem of definition. What exactly counts as a column? Does 'column' refer to all newspaper pieces expressing strong personal opinion – in which case those political essays found in early newspapers, pamphlets and magazines would have to be included? Or should 'column' only refer to pieces which meet contemporary definitions: first-person, opinion-led, short articles with a focus on political and social commentary?

Silvester (1997, p. xi) provides a useful definition in *The Penguin Book of Columnists*: 'In making the distinction between the column and the essay, I have relied upon the following criteria. Firstly the column appears in the same publication on a regular basis, usually in the same position and with the same heading, a by-line and an approximately predictable length.' Secondly, the columnist is conscious of audience in a way the essayist is not. Thirdly – and of particular relevance for this book's arguments – 'the column has sometimes been categorised as 'personal journalism in which the personality of the writer is a self-referential element in the text along with the subject matter. As Hallam Walker Davies put it, in his journalism handbook, *The Column*, "there is one thing all good columns have in abundance. That is the individuality, or "personality" or "ego" of the columnist ... all good columns bear the imprint of the ego of the columnist, an ego that is a live thing, much to be reckoned with" ' (ibid., p. xi).

Hallam Walker Davies' quote comes from 1926, evidence that columns of sorts were a recognised part of the American journalistic landscape at this point, not the political essay typical of early journalism, but other types of authored columns dealing with humorous, literary or local issues. Some of America's great writers of the 1800s made their living this way, including Walt Whitman and Mark Twain. By the 1920s, the column was, according to cultural critic, Gilbert Seldes (1924, p. 277), 'the most sophisticated of the minor arts in America'. But columns in this period were still the domain of humourists and literary or theatrical figures, the most famous including Heywood Broun who wrote a regular column called 'It Seems to Me', Damon Runyan who wrote humorous sketches and H. L. Mencken who wrote mainly on literary subjects.

This period also saw the rise of the gossip columnist. Walter Winchell's journalism began with contributing notes about his acting troupe on backstage bulletin boards. He then started writing for theatre-based and local newspapers, and was eventually hired in 1929 by the *New York Daily Mirror* where he wrote 'On-Broadway', which became the first syndicated gossip column. Powerful and acerbic, he made as many enemies as friends and inspired the columnist portrayed in Alexander MacKendrick's 1957 film, *Sweet Smell of Success*. Various kinds of what we might broadly call lifestyle columns blossomed in this era, not just gossip and entertainment but also fashion and domestic advice, the one area of column writing where women were well represented (Belford 1986).

But what really brought the column to prominence as a genre was the emergence of the political opinion column in America in the 1920s. The *New York World* pioneered a recognisable op-ed page with columnists, although the format was not picked up again until the late 1960s (Socolow 2010). But from 1921, this was the home to Walter Lippmann's first columns. Later he moved to the *New York Herald-Tribune*, where he contributed his long-running column, 'Today and Tomorrow'. Syndicated across America, the column won two Pulitzer Prizes and made Lippmann the most influential, respected and famous political columnist in the world.

Syndication gave American columnists a prominence not enjoyed by their British counterparts. America, being such a vast country, was dominated by regional rather than national newspapers. Lippmann's column was syndicated to regional newspapers because it explained the national political scene in Washington to the remote regions. 'After the first world war the United States was just beginning to confront its destiny as the world's rising great power', writes Marr (2005, p. 353), 'yet most Americans were stuck in relatively ignorant cut-off towns. Lippmann, known as the Moses of Liberalism, helped fill the gap.' Subsequently, the opinion column grew steadily in popularity emerging as, 'the newspaper sensation of the thirties' (Schudson 1978, p. 150). Opinion writing was further boosted by new publications like *Time* magazine which pioneered a blend of fact and opinion.

Many American columnists became rich and powerful but in Britain, without syndication's stimulus, the political column evolved more slowly. Writers largely remained anonymous or pseudonymous through the 1920s and 1930s. James Cameron reflecting on his career described the anonymity which characterised British journalists in the 1930s. 'In those days', he said about his early career at the Courier (Cameron1984), 'it was the custom to have nobody to write under their own name but under a great variety of pseudonyms. In this way I'd change my role and character completely from week to week assuming sometimes the nature of this, sometimes the nature of that. Male or female. Animal, vegetable. Mineral.' But one or two columnists, although using pseudonyms, did become famous and influential, like William Connor, a political and social commentator with a huge following who wrote as Cassandra in the *Daily Mirror* and is still regarded as perhaps the greatest of all newspaper columnists (Shrimsley 2003; Waterhouse 2004).

The Second World War brought journalists to greater personal prominence including James Cameron himself, Martha Gellhorn and Richard Dimbleby. Some columns existed: there was, for example, George Orwell's 'As I please', which he started writing for *Tribune* magazine in 1943. But more typical of British journalism was the special correspondent, whether dealing with industry, home affairs and especially war. By 1947, then writing for the *Daily Express* as a foreign correspondent, Cameron was far from anonymous, having not only a prominent byline but a picture too. The caption read: 'Cameron in de Valera's land – once again James Cameron is in the centre of an unusual political battle – this time just across the Irish channel'. But he was not a columnist in the modern sense and it was not until the 1960s that political columnists became a regular part of British scene led by Henry Fairlie who wrote his 'Political Commentary' column in the *Spectator*, first under the nom de plume 'Trimmer', then under his own byline. Marr (2005, p. 353), giving a vivid account of Fairlie's colourful life as a hard drinker and womaniser, calls him the first 'potential imitator of Lippmann' who helped define the modern British political column.

The slow evolution from correspondent to columnist can be seen in copies of the *Times*. Through the first four decades of the twentieth century it printed 'special articles', often on the index page, usually from relevant but unnamed correspondents and more like the contemporary news feature. In the 1940s, the editorial and letters page were becoming more demarcated, although the layout was still jumbled. There were long parliamentary reports, and rather more interpretative pieces of news all mixed in with humorous or informative pieces on subjects like 'beetles and lettuces'. By the beginning of the 1960s, bylined 'special' articles were more prominent. William Rees-Mogg who became editor in 1967 (Greenslade 2012) created a more recognisably modern format for the editorial consisting of three short leader pieces, letters and an 800-word 'special article'. These were columns in all but name often occupied by regular *Times*' journalists like Louis Heren. In a column entitled, 'More to George Wallace than a racist ticket' (30 July 1968), for example, he advances strong and controversial opinions. During this period Bernard Levin, who Marr describes as a 'shouter', began to appear as the *Times*' first recognisably modern columnist.

By the 1960s, many newspapers were acknowledging the importance of identifiable writers. Named political commentators and correspondents, many of whom wrote regular slots, began to have considerable influence both outside and inside their newspapers. Geoffrey Taylor's *History of The Guardian* (1993) tells of how a labour correspondent like John Cole was able to influence the political direction of the whole newspaper. On the same newspaper, Peter Jenkins, soon to become Britain's best-known political opinion writer, moved from correspondent to commentator. In 1969, the *Guardian* promoted a redesign with adverts foregrounding their 'controversial writers': 'Place in order of preference', it commanded, continuing 'Readers have very individual reactions to Guardian writers – because they're very individual writers. The Guardian encourages them to write like human beings not dictating machines... Alistair Cooke, John Arlott, Norman Shrapnel, Peter Jenkins' (Taylor 1993, p. 179).

Peter Preston, former editor of the *Guardian*, describes the newspaper around the time of this redesign as 'a much smaller paper' which only had 'a much smaller leader page, with one leader article – which was much obsessed over – and the readers' letters. Apart from one column on the back – given to carefully balanced contributors – that was it' (Preston 2013). It was the creation of the *Guardian*'s op-ed pages putting three columns of comment and news analysis on the pages opposite the editorial which embodied the new directions in journalism. The identifiable voice of analysis and commentary was becoming audible, the beginning of an irreversible process by which editorial and commentary effectively reversed size and significance.

Why columns?

Studies of American journalism claim the political column has its roots in the aftermath of the First World War. Editors at the time felt that the post-war climate was uniquely complex and warranted more analytical, opinion-based and explanatory journalism. Schudson argues that, from the 1930s, the political column also represented an implicit recognition that the model of impartial objective facts was not sustainable: 'The political column was, among other things, journalism's most important institutional acknowledgement that there were no longer facts, only individually constructed interpretations' (1978, p. 150). *Time* magazine co-founder, Henry Luce, famously said, 'Show me a man who thinks he's objective and I'll show you a man who's deceiving himself' (cited in Schudson ibid.). Walter Lippmann himself questioned notions of objective reporting. A journalist's version of the truth, he said, is subjective and limited to how he constructs his reality. The press, he claimed, 'deals with a society in which the governing forces are so imperfectly recorded. The theory that the press can itself record those forces is false. It can normally record only what has been recorded for it by the working of institutions. Everything else is argument and opinion, and fluctuates with the vicissitudes, the self-consciousness, and the courage of the human mind' (Lippmann 1921, p. 232). Lipmann believed the press was too fragile to bear the charge as 'an organ of direct democracy'. By contrast, he claimed, the commentator can get behind events and make sense of them: 'the function of news is to signalize an event, the function of truth is to bring to light the hidden facts, to set them in relation with each other, and make a picture of reality on which men can act' (Lippmann 1921, p. 230). Lippmann was one of the first to see clearly the importance of the column for interpretation and analysis of events which he thought was as valuable, if not more so, than any pretence at objective record. George Orwell made the same point about the importance of interpretation when he wrote of his own column: 'to see what is in front of your nose requires a constant struggle' (*Tribune* 22 March 1946).

There were other wider social, technological and cultural factors at work in the shift towards interpretation. Television had a major impact on journalism, felt as early as the 1940s in America and from the late 1950s in the United Kingdom. In America, the arrival of television in the late 1940s and early 1950s caused print publications to rethink their approach in an effort to remain relevant in view of television's superior news-breaking ability and its entertainment values. Out of necessity, journalism became more analytical and opinionated. 'With broadcast newscasts now routinely beating them to breaking news, newspapers increasingly are emphasizing news features and more analytical approaches', (Stephens 1991, p. 277). The arrival of immediate news from outside broadcasting – and later the emergence of rolling news – fuelled the second wave of more opinionated journalism in the 1960s. 'At the end of the sixties', says Peter Preston (2013), 'there was an explosion of television viewing and with it an explosion of news coverage. If you were planning what was going to sell the paper the next day, it couldn't just be the same old news that people had seen the night before on television. If you were going to attract attention on the newsstand, it had to be fresh news, or a fresh take on that news. In news terms you have to do what television can't do. What was missing was interpretation; what does this news mean.'

This was a two-way process. Television needed more flamboyant personalities and recruited the journalists whose personalities were most visible in their writing. In Britain, those who made the transition easily included James Cameron as well as Malcolm Muggeridge, Brian Redhead, Bernard Levin and Margarita Laski. Reciprocally, television influenced journalism by creating an increasing public appetite for a personality attached to words, a person who built trust and rapport by familiarity, visibility and repetition.

Advertising played a role too by fuelling big increases in page numbers and the appearance of consumer lifestyle weekend magazines. Put bluntly these required more copy which could be produced quickly and relatively cheaply. But there were wider changes too (addressed later in this book), which throughout the 1960s meant less conformist, more questioning attitudes towards traditional sources of authority including the newspaper's authoritative, editorial voice. Newspapers began to promote recognisable individuals, as the *Guardian* advert shows. In preference to being told, and explained to, by a remote presence, journalism was embracing the idea of individual interpretation, of disagreement and provocation. Instead of instructing and informing, attention was now on how to engage, and even entertain, readers.

Two newspapers were instrumental in harnessing these trends to create the modern op-ed pages: the *New York Times* on one side of the Atlantic, the *Guardian* on the other. Discussions leading up to the creation of the *NYT* op-ed pages reveal much about why commentary became so significant. The *NYT* op-ed page was launched in 1970, synthesising a number of different precursors, to provide 'greater opportunity for American and foreign writers to put forward their ideas in the form of original signed articles' (cited in Socolow 2010, p. 288). This 'distinctive combination of outsiders and journalists, diverse voices, some art usually a cartoon and some humour, or wider philosophical essays known as the op-ed began a revolution in content and design that swept through America newspapers in 70's' (Green 2011, p. 1). By 1994, nearly half of American newspapers had an op-ed page. John B. Oakes, the editor at time of its launch, had long argued, 'the function of newspapers and newspaper men' was to 'interpret the age to the general public'. However, he opposed the idea of editorials telling readers what to think. Instead he pushed for something more democratic: 'interpretative responsibility' should not mean 'ostentatious representations of authority'; rather 'a good journalist needs to be wary of appearing too professorial, elite and inflexible'. The deepest responsibility of a newspaper, Oakes wrote, was 'the same responsibility the college has for its students – the responsibility of making them think' (Oakes, cited in Socolow 2010, p. 283).

The *New York Times* saw the purpose of the editorial page as questioning and debunking. When the pages were launched, the editors hoped 'that a contribution may be made towards stimulating new thought and provoking new discussion of political problems'. Their news release added: 'points of view in disagreement with the editorial position of the Times will be particularly welcomed' (cited in Socolow 2010, pp. 281, 288). They were true to their word, publishing, for example, voices highly critical of government policy on Vietnam. One such contributor, Chomsky, amusingly grumbled about the impossibility of fitting anything into 700 words. Perhaps he was in their minds when after a while they noted: 'The most successful pieces have been highly individualistic, opinionated and pungent' adding, 'you will not be arrested if the piece is also witty' (cited in Socolow, p. 288).

In the wake of the 1960s, the *New York Times*, the *Washington Post* (from a less conservative position) and other newspapers all worked on their forums of opinion as political conflicts of the period increased, circulation decreased and scepticism towards the received sources of authority increased. The op-ed page was 'a child of its times', said

Harrison Salisbury, one of the editors employed in the launch. He later called the 1960s the era of 'panic button America'. The period, he said, was 'an age of scepticism' in which not one institution in American society escaped re-examination (Cited Socolow 2010, p. 291).

In the United Kingdom, the same process was underway in broadsheets like the *Times* and the *Guardian* where commentary was also becoming increasingly significant. Editorials had begun their slow relegation from voice of the nation to a necessary, but scarcely read, position statement. The *Guardian*, under the editorship of Peter Preston, was particularly significant in determining the shape of comment to come. Like the *New York Times'* op-ed pages, Preston's comment pages acknowledged the increasingly important role of individual interpretation in engaging readership. But in some ways, the *Guardian* pages by the 1980s were more radical. The *NYT* was relatively conservative with a small 'c' in its choice of writers and definition of politics. The *Guardian*, by contrast, widened definitions not just by including feature-based comment but also with the kind of topics and writers involved on the pages. Combined with the way the newspaper embraced a wider social agenda across all its pages, including developing the women's page and expanding arts coverage, there was more of an implicit challenge to the old news hierarchies than in the *NYT*.

Preston talks of absorbing lessons from the tabloid sector which was then shaking up the newspaper world, bringing increasing numbers of readers to newspapers by offering more lifestyle and entertainment coverage. Tabloids throughout the 1980s were also promoting controversial individuals as part of their popularising package. Eccentrics like Royal commentator James Whittaker, columnists like George Gale, John Akass, Jean Rook and writers like John Junor, all cranked up the temperature with their forthright comments. Jean Rook, known as the 'First Lady of Fleet Street', who described herself as having 'clawed and scratched' her way up, was famously savage to other women, while Akass, Gale and Junor dished out highly provocative views. After the IRA bombing of the Brighton hotel where the Conservatives were holding their party conference, Junor wrote: 'With compatriots like these [the IRA Brighton bombers] wouldn't you rather admit to being a pig than be Irish?' a comment which led to him being censured for racism by the Press Council. He was regularly mocked by *Private Eye* but his provocative 'gobby' style was snapped up by radio and TV. Nothing could be further from an impersonal voice of authority. This was like arguing in the pub, with identifiable people, out for a good argument and prepared to be held accountable for their views.

All this was very different from the contributors nourished by, and the format pioneered by, Preston and followed by other broadsheets, for which these kinds of views were anathema. Nevertheless, there were common underlying forces at play, namely the increasing emphasis on distinctive style and personality, aiming to bring readers into more intimate connection with their newspaper by giving voice to the topics and styles of more popular discussion. The story in journalism since, on both sides of the Atlantic, has been of the exponential increase of personal opinionated columns. It has been especially noticeable in British journalism, which is ironic given that Britain was slow to embrace columns. But adopt them it has. Thirty years ago a handful of writers were known for their opinions and most of those because they had transferred, like Levin and Muggeridge, to radio and television. Now there are endless columnists – every newspaper has a stable of them – who, if not quite household names, are at least highly visible in public life – Richard Littlejohn and Peter Hitchens on the *Mail*, George Monbiot, Polly Toynbee and Simon Jenkins on the *Guardian*, Mathew Parris on the *Times*. Columnists have become some of the highest earners in journalism, sometimes traded like footballers, and regularly found on public platforms across the country.

The 'commentariat' as they are called, not entirely flatteringly, are now very influential and have been called 'journalism's aristocracy' (Shrimsley 2003, p. 29). Mathew Parris, Yasmin Alibhai-Brown, Polly Toynbee, Simon Jenkins and George Monbiot all appear regularly in key places where cultural and political policy is debated, namely BBC 4's Today Programme, BBC 2's News Night and high-profile conferences and parliamentary debates. While appearing on such debates does not confer influence – and most British columnists, according to Duff (2008), are extremely modest about the idea that they exercise such influence – nevertheless, a column on a national newspaper is a stepping stone to public prominence. I experienced some of this when writing a regular column for the *Guardian*, where my own ideas were sometimes picked up for the subject of a debate and where invitations often came to take part in discussions on other media. Political columnists, in particular, play a significant role in the 'political public sphere'. A column is a platform into public life; 'it deals the columnist into the national date' (Tunstall 1996, p. 180), so the ideal column is one that 'takes the national conversation forward' (Marr 2005, p. 356).

This is a two-way street. Having a column is a route to influence but high profiles are also advantageous for the newspaper although, as Shrimsley (2003) points out, readers rarely follow a columnist who transfers to another newspaper. Even so, a high-profile columnist can be free publicity for a newspaper or website. 'Columnists are a key part of the paper's overall personality, constituting its intellectual praetorian guard' (Glover 1999, p. 295).The personalities, views and modes of expression on offer reflect the readers back to themselves, signalling 'we are this type of paper'. This is true even when the columnist does not always share the exact political views of their newspapers.

Duff interviewed a number of leading columnists concluding that most had come from rather uniform, heavyweight reporting backgrounds, including even being people of similar background, gender and outlook: the majority 'are cantankerous men of fairly mature years' (Tunstall 1996, p. 177). Wahl-Jorgensen (2008) hints at a top-down establishment nature of columnist's authority, journalists selected as representatives of authorities endorsed by the newspaper. Yet this is not always the case. My own entry, neither male nor from heavyweight reporting is symptomatic of the wider remit and function of the contemporary opinion column. Authority is a factor, in that writers must be trusted to be factually accurate, responsible with material, with a wide range of references – but 'authority' is also derived elsewhere. Columnists aiming primarily at interpretation and distinctive point of view do not have to belong to a uniform type or background. Far from it. What is paramount is interpretation. The columnist's cache is not position or old-fashioned journalistic authority but 'scoops of interpretation', as *Guardian* columnist Hugo Young so aptly described it (Young 2003, p. xvii), together with the ability to connect with and entertain the readership. Comment writers are cherished for provoking strong responses. This is particularly true now with online commentary where writers are valued for the number of hits and responses and for having their views picked up elsewhere on the media, by twitter or in blogs.

This overarching importance of being able to entertain and engage is why polemicists – without particular party political allegiances – flourish. Julie Burchill rose to prominence reviewing for the *New Musical Express* (NME) and was offered a column on the *Sunday Times* where she took provocative and unpredictable views on any number of subjects. A contrarian, she would display her left-wing background, then openly praise Margaret Thatcher, even supporting her hawkish response to the Falkland's crisis. 'If Burchill is famous for anything it is for being Julie Burchill, the brilliant, unpredictable, outrageously outspoken writer who has an iconoclastic, usually offensive, view on everything' (Arlidge *The Observer* 9 June 2002). Burchill is partisan to the point of using her columns to both hero worship and feud. But people read Birchill not just for explication or interpretation but also for performance, uncensored displays of personality and brilliant phrasing, whether at the end they would be cheering or spitting. She once described her writing as 'the writing equivalent of screaming and throwing things' (*Scotland on Sunday* 3 August 2008).

Burchill is a champion example of how personal position and even personality have become key elements in contemporary commentary. Far from getting in the way, personal reaction, personal interpretation and even personal revelations are vital. We've become interested in how ideas belong to the people who express them. Along with social, political and technological elements, this factor is more nebulous but no less important. This is a discourse which instead of telling us what to think invites us to react, whether in agreement or disagreement, to a voice which doesn't stand in the shade but shows its whole personality in turns of phrase, personal characteristics and even emotional life.

Personality has come to prominence, which explains why it's not just political opinion columns which have proliferated. Personal columns are everywhere: me, me, me clamouring from every page. Thirty years ago the columns that existed were mainly addressing political, advice or lifestyle issues. Now there are columnists in every section of the newspaper. Specialist sections all have star columnists like the *Observer*'s Nigel Slater on cooking, or the *Guardian*'s Alys Fowler on gardening. Personal columns have proliferated and they focus not just on the individual's take on the day so much as the individual's day itself. Nigel Slater doesn't just tell us about cooking but about himself. Tim Dowling's column in the *Guardian* weekend, or Liz Jones's diary in the *Daily Mail*'s *You* magazine are not even about lifestyle or social issues in the widest sense, they are just the ongoing narrative of their lives. Columns, says Marr (2005, p. 365), have multiplied crazily in modern British newspapers. 'There are columns on gardens, cheap wine and etymology, columns on bicycling, on "my loveable children", on bird watching, and sex with strangers, columns on every form of activity and dreaming known to urban mankind. There are ghosted columns by celebrities, and columns by celebrities that would have been much better if they had been ghosted'. Columns, he continues, quoting another columnist Keith Waterhouse, 'are now offered "like Sunday school prizes" to TV personalities, pop stars and suchlike minor celebs who have nothing to say'. A few columnists 'are witty enough to write grippingly about almost nothing at all ... but behind these, lumbering desperately and wittering as they lumber, are a thousand no hopers who somehow stumble into print, wasting many an innocent readers time'.

Marr conducted a somewhat unscientific, but useful, count of columnists concluding 'There are by my counting upwards of 200 regular national columnists and twice as many if you add in magazines and local papers. And a huge number of people like me who write occasional pieces'. 'It is a formidable babble of finger jabbing, shrugging, winking, frowning, hectoring verbiage and a small industry in its own right' (p. 366). Marr's contempt shows through in these comments and in his explanations for the proliferation: columns exist as a cheap ways of filling pages, and because they promote the consumer lifestyle which sustains commercial press. Such contempt is widespread. 'They fill the space on demand, they are (usually) reliable, and as long as they are fed and watered, they are not as a rule much trouble. But they spread like the conifer forests from which they breed. Pass the chainsaw' (Waterhouse 2004, p. 7). Peter Wilby decries 'the rise of a commentariat who express opinions that have no basis in knowledge' (New Statesman, 13 March,1996). Few give the impression, says Shrimsley (2003, p. 30), 'that they stray far from their ivy clad manors'. Martin Kettle alleges political columnists sometimes 'pursue their trade unencumbered by either experience or the facts' (*The Guardian* 17 December 2002).

John Lloyd (2005) complains of columnists crowding our more important kinds of journalism, namely reporting. And there's widespread agreement that there are too many undeserving. 'It's a plain statement of fact', Marr laments (2005, p. 375), 'that we have too many columnists ... (it) is evidence of social sickness'. Silvester (1997) concludes that the 'British press is overpopulated with second rate performers'. And according to these critics, the Internet with its reliance on the personal column or blog is the apotheosis of all their fears, nothing authoritative, only 'a cacophony of rival voices' (Young 2003, p. xvi).

Such criticisms come from old-fashioned, sober notions of journalism, involving conservative notions of appropriate material for newspapers – again usually conventional politics and reportage. They fail to understand the proliferation of the personal column is not in and of itself antipathetic to responsible and accountable journalism. The ability to see where views are coming from, and to interrogate the personality and the stance that produced them, can be not only more entertaining and engaging but also more transparent. 'People do not take anonymous editorials or "leaders" as seriously as they used to', says Marr (2005, p. 368). 'They've lost faith in the Olympian voice of authority. Much research and good argument can still flow through an editorial. What has gone wrong for them is that readers have lost respect for the idea of anonymous or institutional authority passed down through newspaper generations.' Reflecting on the rise of the column he adds, 'we are used to putting names to ideas, and to watching contradictions emerge as a particular writer struggles with the world; that seems more honest these days than anonymous, corporate lines of opinion. Today's readers are more sceptical and consumerist than post-war generations who turned to leaders to know what to think; they are likelier to argue back, at least mentally. The fall of the editorial and the rise of the columnist are like the collapse of late medieval Catholic dogma before a rag tag collection of itinerant roadside preachers'.

'The truth is that amid the noisome banality of wall-to-wall news', says Simon Jenkins writing of fellow columnist Christopher Hitchens (*The Guardian* 16 December 2011) 'strong opinion and passionate conviction expressed in grammatical prose can still draw the crowds'. This is to do with knowing who is speaking, where views are coming from and a preference for seeing a recognisable individual create a distinctive, clever and amusing argument, rather than passively accepting a disembodied voice pronouncing on the events of the day. The essence of successful contemporary columnists is not to hide themselves but to display themselves through distinctive writing inviting response. 'It can be as abrasive as Littlejohn', says Keith Waterhouse (2004, p. 11), 'as urbane as Simon Jenkins, as mynah bird mocking as Craig Brown, as brittle as Julie Burchill, but it has to have a style so recognisable that it doesn't really need a by-line. Which is? As Louis Armstrong used to say about jazz, if you have to ask, you haven't got it'.

3 Gonzo and I: The New Journalism

The previous chapters have pointed to journalists and journalism falling outside strict conventions of 'objective' reporting even while remaining attached to ideals of truthfulness, accuracy and facticity. But the writing mentioned so far was not particularly 'theorised' and certainly did not come out of any explicit, agenda-led movement, or 'alternative' tradition. That changed in America in the 1960s. 'The New Journalism' as it came to be known, associated with writers including Hunter S. Thompson, Tom Wolfe, Truman Capote, Gay Talese and Joan Didion, was the first time a diverse group of contemporaneous journalists recognised themselves as engaged in the roughly similar activity of challenging the straightjacket of objective journalism.

Although 'New Journalism' is by no means the 'subjective' writing as we now see in confessional journalism or blogging, it nevertheless deserves a place at the centre of this book. This is because, along with problematising the conventions of traditional journalism, one of New Journalism's most striking aspects is the centrality of the personal voice, either through direct use of 'I' or by employing such distinctive style it presents as the personal identity of the author. This was the first time journalists self-consciously included themselves in the picture. It was also a significant moment where issues associated with subjectivity, that is emotional issues and reactions, including the journalist's own, became valid subject matter. For the themes of this book then, New Journalism is significant. It gives the first clear sighting of the social and cultural forces pushing for the inclusion of more personal material as well as the first airing of ethical and formal issues which now attach to this material.

Origins

It was Tom Wolfe who first formulated the ideas associated with this writing when in 1973 he introduced a selection of articles and excerpts from the previous decade in a collection entitled *The New Journalism* (Wolfe and Johnson 1973). Although Wolfe insisted he didn't know who had first used the name or kick-started the movement, it was this collection which saw the term established in general consciousness. In his introduction, Wolfe made it clear he thought this writing posed more of a challenge to the idea of 'literature', especially to the cultural pre-eminence of the novel, than to journalism. Wolfe claimed all journalists, like much of the wider population, fantasised about one day writing a great novel. Even the so-called new journalists were still in thrall to this ambition even as they began to write a new kind of more literary journalism. 'They never guessed for a minute', Wolfe said, that 'the work they would do over the next ten years, as journalism, would wipe out the novel as literature's main event' (1973, p. 20).

Wolfe was right that New Journalism had a lasting impact on publishing taste but not, as he imagined, by displacing the novel's cultural pre-eminence. The legacy has been more to do with undermining old journalistic certainties and conventions while simultaneously popularising new forms of non-fiction writing. This writing has taken different paths in America and Britain but is now known variously as 'literary journalism', 'creative non-fiction', 'narrative non-fiction'. The lack of an agreed title reflects its hybridity, both in form and content. But, whatever its name, it now has a huge presence on the publishing scene. Narrative non-fiction, taking in anything from journalist John Grogan's memoir of his badly behaved dog, *Marley and Me* (2008) to Edmund de Waal's *The Hare with the Amber Eyes* (2011), regularly dominates best-seller lists.

Recently, literary journalism scholarship has reclaimed as forebears of New Journalism the many early reporters and journalists who departed from strictly impartial writing and used more literary forms including the personal voice (including some discussed in Chapter 1). Norman Sims (2008) however suggests the more direct antecedents emerged in America in the 1940s and 1950s, especially a number of writers associated with the *New Yorker* magazine whose themes, preoccupations and stylistic devices anticipated New Journalism. A.J. Leibling's work is particularly striking. He moved easily between foreign reporting, like his coverage of the Second World War, and intimate portraits of aspects of American life which he loved such as Broadway lowlife and boxing. But he also self-consciously included himself in his journalism and often questioned beliefs in journalistic objectivity. His personality and interests were always so much in the foreground that his journalism has been described as extended autobiography.

Other contenders include John Hersey whose *Hiroshima*, published in 1946, told the story of the atomic bomb through the lives of ordinary Japanese people. At a time when hostilities with Japan were still fresh in the public mind, this article was a powerful reminder, through its personal and intimate focus, of the American readership's shared humanity with the Japanese. Lillian Ross was another well-respected contributor to the *New Yorker* who is particularly remembered for her devastating portrait of Hemingway, a cult figure at the time. In 1950 Ross portrayed him as something of a rambling drunk in a relatively unmediated account of two days spent in his company.

Joseph Mitchell's articles have also been singled out by Sims as important precursors of New Journalism. Mitchell is praised for taking readers into the inner life of characters as in *The Old House at Home* (*New Yorker* 1940) a long piece about a New York bar told through several generations of characters who had inhabited it. Mitchell imagines how they lived and what they said, and weaves together what he's been told with what he imagines about their preoccupations and motives. In *Old Mr Flood*, one of three pieces about New York's fish market, he went further, creating a composite character. 'Mr. Flood', he admitted later, 'is not one man; combined in him are aspects of several old men who work or hang out in Fulton Fish Market, or who did in the past' (Sims 2008, p. 173).

For today's tastes, Mitchell's writings, though memorable, are problematic in this aspect. Few journalists would find composite characters acceptable. New Journalism eschewed such devices as contrary to true reportage and British journalists has always baulked at the imagined dialogues characteristic of this kind of early literary journalism. But Mitchell remains highly regarded for his vivid portrayals of certain types of people, and their emotional life, usually neglected by journalism: 'You're trying to report', Mitchell once said, 'without knowing it, the unconscious and the conscious of characters' (Sims 2008, p. 175). Mitchell wrote one of his most famous pieces about the bohemian, Joe Gould, who had liked to interview ordinary people, and claimed he was inspired by Yeats' belief that 'the history of a nation is not in parliaments and battlefields but in what the people say to each other on fair days and high days and in how they farm and quarrel and go on pilgrimage' (cited in Mitchell's article 'Professor Seagull'. *New Yorker* 12 December 1942, p. 28). It was this interest in ordinary lives which prefigured aspects of New Journalism

While earlier authors like Mitchell elevated the ordinary and put more style and self-expression into their journalism, nevertheless their writing was the exception rather than the rule. The Second World War had been 'a hard news event filled with death and disaster on a historic scale' (Sims 2008, p. 164) during which the news style of objectivity dominated. As a result, this more individualistic self-expression didn't have a ready place in the post-war period. This was a conformist decade and so was most of the journalism produced; even these so-called forebears of New Journalism have a cosy, folksy nostalgic feel to them. By contrast, the writers who burst on the scene in the 'blazingly non-conformist' days of the 1960s (Sims 2008, p. 163) saw themselves in direct conflict with the establishment. When the New Journalism emerged, the writers defined themselves by rejecting previous decades and saw themselves as 'political', with a small 'p' certainly and often, like Hunter S. Thompson, with a big 'P' too. Immersed in the maelstrom of the era, the ordinary voices these writers chose to reflect (including their own) were the voices of protest, the voices of a social revolution.

New Journalism's exact timeline and characteristics are vague. Writing in 1973 Ronald Weber said 'Tom Wolfe says he doesn't know who coined the term – or when it was coined – and if he doesn't know probably no-one does. For one decent working definition of the New Journalism is that it's what Tom Wolfe writes' (Weber 1974, p. 13). Tom Wolfe was not only one of the most distinctive, experimental writers in the early 1960s but also was the first to theorise it: 'Wolfe has for some years now been its major theorist and among its most visible practitioners' (ibid.). Many critics attribute New Journalism's genesis to a provocative article Wolfe wrote in 1965 attacking the *New Yorker* magazine. His article, if not exactly a manifesto, certainly threw down the gauntlet to conventional journalism.

Wolfe had become a reporter on the *New York Herald-Tribune* in 1962. He was also one of the two staff writers, the other being Jimmy Breslin (another leading figure in New Journalism) on *New York* magazine. The editor of this new supplement thought that the *New Yorker*, so revered by the literary establishment, was deadly dull and asked Wolfe to take up the theme. Wolfe leapt at it, writing an all-out attack on the magazine entitled 'Tiny Mummies! The True Story of The Ruler of 43rd Street's Land of the Walking Dead!' (Wolfe 1965). It was Wolfe's thesis, says David Remnick (*New York Review of Books* 2 March 1995), editor of the *New Yorker* since 1998, that the magazine at that point had devolved into 'a humourless, genteel museum piece of middlebrow culture'. Wolfe's article was 'a two part pie in the face'.

The article provoked fury but enhanced Wolfe's already growing reputation as a writer. This was confirmed when, shortly after, he published a collection of his essays under the title *The Kandy-Kolored Tangerine-Flake*

Streamline Baby (Wolfe 1965). The articles were about 1960s culture, Wolfe describing the book as 'a non-fiction story of the hippie era'. The collection was radical not just because of its colourful language, direct address and chunks of dialogue, but also for its subjects. Wolfe had turned his back on predictable newsworthy subjects and instead immersed himself in the intimate lives of the counterculture. The book was a best-seller and established Wolfe as a leading figure in the literary experiments that became known as New Journalism. In the next three years he went on to produce two more best-sellers, *The Pump House Gang* (1968) and *The Electric Kool-Aid Acid Test* (1968).

But Wolfe was right to reject the position of founding father and originator of the term when there were many other contenders. 'New Journalism' was already in use in the 1960s and 1970s referring to what Wolfe preferred to describe as 'some sort of artistic excitement in journalism' (Weber 1974). This artistic excitement was the coincidental appearance of a number of writers, all, like Wolfe himself, experimenting with doing journalism differently. By 1965 Norman Mailer had already produced a piece for *Esquire* about the 1960 Democratic Convention, which some claim is really the first piece of New Journalism, while Truman Capote was also working on *In Cold Blood* which became the movement's iconic book. Gay Talese had published a series of extraordinary articles for *Esquire*, and Hunter S. Thompson was poised in 1965 to publish his book on the Hells Angels which has been seen as synonymous with New Journalism ever since. In California, Joan Didion was already writing the magazine articles which were published in 1968 in another iconic collection, *Slouching towards Jerusalem*.

Most of these were feature writers working for magazines like *True*, *New York* and *Esquire*, all straining at the conventions of not just news reporting but feature writing too. They were looking for new subjects and new ways of talking about them. Tom Wolfe described them in characteristic language: 'Young reporters refused to remain laptop dummies who lip-synched the institutional voice of the newspapers. They demanded they were the ones close to the action, editors saw them as disrespectable, lazy, not prepared to accept their professional responsibilities' (cited Pauly 1990, p. 114). In retrospect, says Sims, it's evident that 'Journalism's crisis of authority echoes similar crises throughout American society' (Sims 2008, p. 220). In the same way, as the legitimacy of traditional authority was questioned across society as a whole, so too in journalism. This was particularly focused around America's involvement in Vietnam which created 'a credibility crisis', especially in relation to the 'truth's proffered by professional journalism' (ibid.)

which at the time was failing to challenge the government's version of events.

The writing of these 'new journalists' was defined not by a political agenda so much as by a shared rejection of how journalism was before. It was characterised by the willingness of the authors to expose themselves to scrutiny, the rejection of traditional notions of impartiality often leading to the immersion in the subject and characters and a new approach to storytelling. These writers used techniques and stylistic devices usually associated with fiction, including extended use of direct conversations; a focus on 'real people' as opposed to the 'lofty' subjects of traditional journalism; a new approach to research in the form of extended participant observation; and a different approach to storytelling with the story unfolding rather than being delivered in condensed form, like news, at the beginning. Tom Wolfe (1973, pp. 46–47) picked out four key characteristics: scene-by-scene construction, resorting as little as possible to sheer historical narrative; witnessing as many of these scenes as possible through 'saturation' reporting and 'recording dialogue in full'; use of third-person viewpoint, the technique of presenting every scene to the reader through the eyes of a particular character giving the reader the experience of being inside the character's mind; and recording details that might be symbolic of people's status in life, meaning 'the entire pattern of behaviour and possessions through which people express their position in the world or what they think it is, or what they hope it to be'.

Robert Vare (2000) says these devices are, in a nutshell, the reason why it's proved difficult to agree a fixed and lasting name for this writing. Essentially 'it's a hybrid form, a marriage of the art of storytelling and the art of journalism, an attempt to make drama out of the observable world of real people, real places and real events. It's a sophisticated form of nonfiction writing, possibly the highest form that harnesses the power of facts to the techniques of fiction constructing a central narrative, setting scenes, depicting multidimensional characters and, most importantly, telling the story in a compelling voice that the reader will want to hear'.

As if to illustrate this point, Norman Mailer, coming to journalism from fiction, was one of the first to blur the lines. 'Superman comes to the Supermarket', written for *Esquire* magazine in November 1960, was a piece of long form journalism ostensibly about the Democratic Party Convention. When he wrote it, Mailer was already famous for his novel, *The Naked and the Dead* (1948), based on his experiences during the Second World War. In the *Esquire* piece, he used novelistic techniques and explored novelistic themes of author consciousness. He focused not so much on what was happening as what he thought and felt about events. He reported on who made the speeches and described the demonstrations and the crowds, but the events got submerged into his own interpretations: 'Mailer was one of the first examples of what would become a staple of the New Journalism; the writer who believes that what he observes has no substance outside what has been filtered through his own psyche' (Sims 2008, p. 226).

This piece self-consciously explored the question of the role of the writer himself in his journalism. In one passage, Mailer describes his interview with John F. Kennedy. Instead of focusing on world historical events, Kennedy's policies, or his impressions of the man, Mailer homed in on the fact that Kennedy had raised the subject of Mailer's own novels. 'What struck me most about the interview was a passing remark whose importance was invisible on the scale of politics but was altogether meaningful to my particular competence.' More specifically, Kennedy mentioned Mailer's novel, *Deer Park*, 'which most others don't'. Mailer's ego was flattered. 'If one is to take the worst and assume that Kennedy was briefed for this interview...it still speaks well for the striking instincts of his advisers' (Mailer 1976, pp. 23–24).

Conventional journalism faced with politically significant interviews would exclude personal material, but Mailer lingered on how it affected his impressions of Kennedy, then proceeded to an incisive critique of traditional 'impartial' journalism. He compares the different modes of perception of the novelist and journalist, criticising journalism's assumption that 'the best instrument for measuring history is a faceless, even mindless recorder' (ibid.). By contrast he applauds novelists who filter material through their own perception which, if gathered together in some integrity, can be called style: 'the writer of fiction is moving closer to the world of Einstein. There the velocity of the observer is as crucial to the measurement as the object observed' (ibid., p. ix).

A few years later in *Armies of the Night*, an account of the anti-Vietnam protests then sweeping America, Mailer's involvement in the story tipped over into actual participation. A friend persuaded him to join the protests. Not only did he join but also went to the front and became the second person, of hundreds, to be arrested. As it turned out, far from compromising his view, his partisanship enhanced his insight into the hatred of authority motivating the young people on the marches. 'On the march he is reporter, analyst, impressionist', writes Peter Lennon (*The Guardian* 25 January 2003). 'He exposes America's ignorance and fear; brutality and evil, decency and foolhardy heroism.

He reflects on the hatred of authority among the young generation X.' 'Authority was the manifest of evil to this generation', wrote Mailer, 'The authority had operated on their brain with commercials and washed their brain with packaged education, packaged politics. Authority had lied. It lied through the teeth of corporation executives and cabinet officials and police enforcement officers and newspaper editors and in its mass magazines where the subtlest apologies for the disasters of the authority... were grafted in the best possible style into the ever-open mind of the walking American lobotomy: the corporation office worker and his high-school son' (cited in Lennon ibid.). The ultimate irony of *Armies of the Night* was that Mailer, having been arrested early on and locked up, missed the main event. Yet his book, capturing the mentality of the movement, still won the Pulitzer prize. New Journalism, says Sims (2008, p. 229) 'had challenged the sacred totem of objectivity'.

However, it was another book, already in preparation in the early 1960s, which has been called the real harbinger of the movement. In 1959, after spotting a brief news item about the murder of a family in a distant rural community in Kansas, Truman Capote started working on what would become *In Cold Blood*. The finished book was eventually published in 1966 and remains, as well as New Journalism's iconic text, one of the great works of literature of the twentieth century. It is also a book which posed, in an extreme form, the key ethical dilemmas which now haunt today's more personalised and intimate journalism, namely what are journalists' rights and responsibilities with other people's lives.

In Cold Blood offers a factual account of real events, but it reads like the very best kind of fiction, with all the unfolding drama and tension of a novel. Capote has described in an interview how he spotted a classic piece of news writing about the horrific murder of the respectable Clutter family, in a small rural town in Kansas: it was just 'the bare facts' he said (Weber 1974), but, attracted by the 'strange ordinariness' of the crime, he felt he could write a story about the effect on the small town, the whys and wherefores, the reactions. His eye, he said, was on literary and artistic achievement, looking to write something which would be universal and endure.

Capote travelled to the town with Harper Lee, a childhood friend who had just finished writing *To Kill a Mockingbird*, for which she later became famous. At a loose end, she agreed to be his research assistant. They arrived two days after the funeral and immersed themselves in the community, quite an achievement for a flamboyant homosexual in small town America at that time. Capote had no idea whether the killers would ever be caught, his plan being simply to see how the murder played out in the community. But in March two young killers were caught, and after a swift trial, were found guilty. Capote switched focus to the killers and, retained that focus for the four years the 'boys' were on death row, Capote visited them regularly, becoming, in the case of Perry at least, his only friend. Capote waited until what he always thought would be the inevitable conclusion – their hanging – to complete the narrative.

While Capote did not literally include himself in the text, the book has a strong personal voice. It is beautifully written and constructed and Capote's voice can be heard in the distinctive, powerful individual style. Capote's personal presence in this story is also the elephant in the room, ethically speaking. His involvement with the boys was intense. He visited them regularly in prison bringing them things they requested. By the end, he was Perry's only visitor and was known to think that Perry wasn't evil and should not have been hung. But other than bearing witness to their stories, he did little to help avert their fate. After their execution and the book's publication, Kenneth Tynan launched a blistering attack in the *Observer*, arguing that Capote failed to help the accused. 'We are talking, in the long run, about responsibility; the debt that a writer arguably owes to those who provide him – down to the last autobiographical parentheses – with his subject matter and his livelihood ... For the first time an influential writer of the front rank has been placed in a position of privileged intimacy with criminals about to die, and – in my view – done less than he might have to save them. The focus narrows sharply down on priorities: does the work come first, or does life? An attempt to help (by supplying new psychiatric testimony) might easily have failed: what one misses is any sign that it was ever contemplated. He sacrificed them for money' (*The Observer* 13 March 1966).

Authenticity, another issue which has become increasingly pressing as journalism deals with more intimate emotional issues, was also an issue in the reception of *In Cold Blood*. Controversially, Capote never used note taking, claiming he was an obsessive researcher and had trained himself to have perfect recall of what people said (Weber 1974, p. 194). Some critics thought he had possibly falsified, or at least been overly creative with, his reconstructed dialogues, something that will never be proved since he also destroyed all his notes. This representation of the other is always an issue within journalism. These are real people, not fictional characters and journalism promises facticity and truthfulness about those encounters. There are conventions within so-called objective news reporting which to some extent lessen the tension and reduce the possibility of ethical conflict: the journalist is charged with only reporting truthfully and accurately what is said to him or her; in conventional 'objective' journalism, journalists do not take a position on what someone says to them nor do they speculate on or interpret a source's motivation. As soon as journalists move into different territory, beginning to explore psychological motivation, background and filling in things that they have not strictly speaking witnessed, they enter a different realm, no longer just about the accuracy of the words but also the accuracy of character, impressions and interpretation. *In Cold Blood* was one of the first works which threw up all those questions that have become increasingly pressing in intimate, personal journalism.

If Capote's aim was to disappear, Hunter S. Thompson occupied the opposite end of the scale. From the moment he burst on the scene, the character of Hunter S. was an unavoidable presence. Constitutionally and intellectually oppositional, Thompson was another writer who was uncontainable within the limits of conventional journalism. Unlike some of the others, Thompson had only had a brief spell as a conventional reporter and then as a sports writer. In his early career, he was sacked from virtually every newspaper that employed him until his first major pieces like The Big Sur – about Californian counterculture – brought him to public attention as a fiery, flamboyant writer with a powerful relentless, garrulous voice.

In 1965, Thompson was commissioned to write a piece about his experiences with the California-based Hell's Angels motorcycle club. The Hell's Angels, at the time, were the subject of a classic moral panic in America, feared as criminal and immoral, especially by conservatives. After the *Nation* published Thompson's article on the subject (17 May 1965), he received several book offers and spent the next year living and riding with the Hell's Angels. The resulting book, *Hell's Angels: The Strange and Terrible Saga of the Outlaw Motorcycle Gangs* (Thompson 1967), was a classic piece of anthropological journalism involving total immersion in the culture studied just as the anthropologist is meant to live with the culture he or she is studying, suspending all views and opinions to fully understand what the culture means to the people inside it. Thompson, however, made no attempt to hide his persona. Indeed, the book often digresses into Thompson's inner monologue about his relationship with the Hell's Angels pondering over such questions as whether to share his beer with them or hide it from them. Their relationship was always touchy and broke down when the bikers accused Thompson of exploiting them for personal gain and demanded a share of profits from his writings. They fell out so badly that Thompson was beaten up by a group of Hell's Angels after a party, an event which he then used for promoting and publicising his book.

Thompson's writing is personal in every sense – a wild roller coaster of style, full of allusions, abrupt transitions, fantasies and digressions. But it is also personal in that Hunter S. is fully present in the story from the start, so much so that, as often remarked, it is Thompson who is the real story. Thompson's article The Kentucky Derby is Decadent and Depraved (Thompson 1970) is a perfect illustration of this and is a work as gripping today as when first written. The horse race detains Thompson for a few lines, the piece digressing from the start about his difficulties in getting press accreditation, how to get access to the free press bar as well as about his fortuitous pairing up with Ralph Steadman, a British cartoonist whose capacity for drink and other stimulants led to a lifetime friendship. The piece very rapidly becomes an account of their debauched weekend. Yet in spite of the totally personal preoccupations, the piece delivers cutting insight into the event and the people who go. At one moment, he stares into a mirror and studies his own debauched, drink- and drug-raddled face. This is the moment of understanding what the event is really about for the race goers, since he has become one of them and given in to the same impulses. Far more than any 'objective' commentary on the occasion, Thompson's personal immersion and self-reflection deliver a much more insightful account. This is not a journalist standing outside his subject but a journalist right inside it: Steadman and he are as annihilated, probably more so, than the racegoers they had come to report on.

The Kentucky Derby is often held up as pure 'Gonzo', the meaningless name Steadman is said to have given Thompson's version of New Journalism. Gonzo is highly subjective journalism, point of view gone wild, mixing fantasy and memoir together with a foregrounded subjective, albeit addled, consciousness. Thompson never espoused the idea of journalistic detachment in the first place but by the time he produced his finest book, *Fear and Loathing in Las Vegas* (1971), it was an irrelevance. *Fear and Loathing* grabs the reader by the throat and doesn't let go, a wild trip with Thompson off his head on a cocktail of drugs, ranting about politics, America and journalism itself.

Thompson is a brilliant writer, highly entertaining as well as gripping, who had much to say about the politics and media of the time. But it was by exploring his own subjectivity that he revealed those times. He may have been the real story of all his journalism, but the story he was writing was the story of the times, the changing consciousness brought about by the counterculture. When sociologists or social theorists look back to understand that period, it's not impartial reportage which sheds light on that era but the passions, preoccupations and consciousness of the people involved in new movements. This is why exploring consciousness, desires, experiences and feelings can make personal journalism so much more significant than the mere introspection it is sometimes accused of being.

Although any of the three authors I've looked at so far – Mailer, Capote and Thompson – could justifiably be called the first 'new journalist', it was another writer altogether who, in 1973, Wolfe uses to illustrate his own first electrifying encounter with New Journalism. The article which drew Wolfe's attention so forcefully was one which employed techniques of fiction (scene-by-scene narrative, drama and direct speech) to create its immediate and gripping effect. Wolfe, in typical style, recounts his reactions to this new writing: '*What inna namea Christ is this* in the fall of 1962 I happened to pick up a copy of *Esquire* and read a story called "Joe Louis: the King as a middle aged man"'. The piece, said Wolfe, didn't open like an ordinary magazine article at all. It opened with the tone and mood of a short story, with a rather intimate scene, or intimate by the standards of magazine journalism in 1962. The piece could have been turned into a non-fiction short story with very little effort. Indeed Wolfe initially wondered if the author had 'made the whole thing up' (Wolfe 1973, p. 23). He notes the irony of this thought, since this accusation was one which came to be made in a more sustained way against most of the practitioners of New Journalism, including Wolfe.

The article in question was by Gay Talese, then mainly writing features for *Esquire* magazine. Talese is best known for his groundbreaking article 'Frank Sinatra Has a Cold', which ran in April 1966 and was once named the 'best story *Esquire* ever published'. In the winter of 1965, Talese had been sent on commission by *Esquire* to Los Angeles to profile Sinatra. But Sinatra was under the weather – he did indeed have a cold – and refused to be interviewed. So Talese hung around Sinatra's haunts and associates filling in the background and circumstances to Sinatra's life. The article he produced remains the most insightful portrait of Frank Sinatra and still one of the best profiles ever written. Talese didn't 'hide' in the piece. Instead he builds into the piece his own position as a sort of hanger on, moving around with all the others, something which enhances his perceptions of Sinatra rather than compromising them.

Like many of his contemporaries, Talese believed in total immersion in his subject and in reportage based on close observation or, more accurately, participation. He was often scathing about journalists who stayed put in their offices, speaking to a couple of people then knocking out an article. By contrast, Talese believed that to know a subject you had to put yourself fully inside it. In Talese's case, however, his 'big' project happened to be about sexual mores – investigating how Americans' sexual morality had changed in the wake of the 1960s. His participation in his subject meant his personal life, in particular his marriage, came under painful public scrutiny.

Talese is still with Nan Ahearn who he married in 1959. She came from a wealthy cultured family, moved in literary circles and went on to forge a high-powered career as one of New York's most influential editors working for Random House and then as an agent which remains her profession; she represents many leading novelists including Ian McEwan. Talese and Nan were, and still are, a New York power couple, but in 2009 the *New Yorker* described their relationship as 'this legendary literary marriage in all its baroque complexity' (Jonathan Van Meter *New York Review of Books* 26 April 2009). The roots of this 'baroque complexity' lie in Talese's New Journalism, more specifically in his book *Thy Neighbor's Wife*, published finally in 1981, the result of years of research. It was a book about 'swingers', nudist colonies and wife swapping and the research was conducted – in true New Journalism style – by immersion in the culture. Talese even went so far, it has been suggested, as sleeping with his neighbour's wife and running massage parlours in New York. 'Fair or not', wrote Van Meter (op. cit.), 'it is a commonly held opinion in publishing circles that Talese's career can be pretty much divided into pre- and post-*Thy Neighbor's Wife* – that the writer and his gift never fully recovered from the shock waves'.

From the perspective of our own times, it's hard to imagine why a book like this would cause such controversy, but wife swapping and orgies and massage parlours were shocking to most people and especially to the establishment figures who surrounded the couple. Talese remains indignant to this day that the 'seriousness' of his subject was misunderstood. He had been wanting to detail how much sexual attitudes had changed America. But stories circulated about how Talese had well and truly crossed the line from a subject he studied to a lifestyle he'd adopted. His wife was questioned about whether she'd participated too. At the time, it was scandalous and Talese made throwaway comments which did nothing to dispel rumours; 'ever since Gay Talese opened the door to their personal lives in the early seventies he invited in all manner of speculation' (Van Meter op. cit.). The scandal meant Talese's book was not well received and he endured many years in the literary wilderness. Recently, the book was republished with a foreword by feminist

Katie Roiphe and was received as having stood the test of time by charting what turned out to have been a seismic shift in sexual attitudes. However, in the afterword, Talese tells how Nan had to accompany him on talk shows 'to explain that our marital love had remained unthreatened while I conducted research in NY massage parlours and a hedonistic nudist colony in LA, which is only half true' (Van Meter op. cit.).

But in spite of the evident pitfalls of personal involvement, Talese has continued to mine his own life. In 1992, he published the first of a three-part autobiography, *Unto the Sons*, a classic of the genres into which literary journalism has largely morphed, memoir, family history and autobiography. *A Writer's Life* followed in 2006, where he writes about the implications for his own life of his immersive journalism, including touching on the 'traumatic event' of *Thy Neighbor's Wife*. Talese is said to be writing the final part, a book explicitly about his marriage. Although not yet published, in interviews he has admitted more about the real problems *Thy Neighbor's Wife* created for his family. He claims he will switch to a third-person narrator when telling the story of his wife's unhappiness and has hinted he may ask her to write her own version. Meanwhile, in a separate interview, his daughter described the painful dilemmas created for the family by the book. The ongoing fallout from *Thy Neighbor's Wife* throws into relief the ethical conundrum of including yourself in the story.

Perhaps of all the writers associated with New Journalism, Joan Didion is the most self-absorbed. In many of her most famous pieces she all but abandoned any kind of third-person journalistic voice, replacing it instead with a highly personalised style which, even when not specifically referring to her own situation or her own feelings, always puts her right in the front of her subject. *Slouching Towards Jerusalem*, published in 1961, was a collection of her magazine articles and opens with the telling comment that 'since I am neither a camera eye nor much given to writing pieces which do not interest me, whatever I write reflects, somewhat gratuitously how I feel' (Didion 1961, p. 13). Her tone is very different from much New Journalism, more introspective and mournful with none of the pyrotechnics of some other writers. Nevertheless it powerfully evokes her subjects and the times she was writing in. California, where Didion lived then, was the epicentre of the cultural and psychological changes shaking America and like Hunter S. Thompson, by foregrounding her own emotions and involvement, she somehow communicates a more profound understanding of the changing environment, mores and preoccupations than more impartial descriptions.

One of the pieces in this collection, 'Some Dreamers of the Golden Dream', has interesting parallels and differences from Capote's *In Cold Blood*. It, too, is a story of a murder committed in a small town, based on another brief item in a tabloid papers, this time about a woman, Lucille Miller, accused of murdering her husband. But there the similarities end. Although the woman is found guilty, Didion remains equivocal. The piece is, as she opens it, 'a story about love and death in the golden land and begins with the country' (Didion 1961, p. 19). Her approach is to get under the skin of the protagonists, those people who have followed their dream to California; her aim is to find their pulse. 'Banyan Street, this is the street that Lucille Miller took.... Of course she came from somewhere else, came off the prairie in search of something she had seen in a movie or heard on the radio, for this is a Southern California story' (ibid., p. 23).

Like the other writers, this journalism reads more like fiction. It sets scenes, creates mood, attributes thoughts and motives to characters. It is based on interviews but does not quote directly or attribute sources. Instead Didion evokes mood – the ennui, the stultifying climate and the claustrophobic society producing people on the make but unable to make it: 'October is the bad month for the wind, the month when breathing is difficult and the hills blaze up spontaneously. There has been no rain since April. Every voice seems a scream' (ibid., p. 19). The story is filtered through Didion's highly personal perspective, her own preoccupations and moods. As she says of her time in California; 'I didn't even know what I wanted to find out. I just hung around and made a few friends' (ibid., p. 95).

Most of Didion's subsequent pieces focus on her own feelings, often of disconnection and sometimes malaise and depression. In *The White Album* (1979), she describes her nervous breakdown. Her extreme introspection alienates some readers since every flicker of her own emotions is captured, dressed up and 'written'. She's a highly stylised writer aware of the artistry of her writing as much as the need to represent her subject. Yet her writing demonstrates again how self-aware, self-conscious writing can sometimes convey a greater awareness of the subject than more conventional reportage. If what is at stake is consciousness, as it was in California in the 1960s, the consciousness was where to be. Not surprisingly, given her highly introspective writing, of all the new journalists, Didion has morphed effortlessly into the confessional writer of contemporary journalism. In *A Year of Magical Thinking* (2005), she has applied the same relentless scrutiny to herself in the year after her husband's sudden death while simultaneously caring for her sick daughter. There can be no more powerful book on grief and memory which although profoundly personal is profoundly universal, proof that sometimes the more personal you become, the more universal you are.

Conclusion

Eason (1984) has divided New Journalism up into two camps: the ethnographers like Wolfe, Talese and Capote who provided an account of 'what it is that's going on in here' and those who saw life through their own filters, like Didion, Mailer and Thompson, who 'focussed on their own realities and even questioned their own ability to grasp reality' (Sims 2008, p. 245). Yet the boundaries between these approaches are blurred. They were all, through different means, raising similar issues, namely tackling more intimate material whether through immersing themselves in a particular culture or consciousness, or through exploring their own reactions to material, or both. These writers challenged conventional ideas of journalism as delivering truth in a detached and impartial way, exposing the fallacies of objectivity and challenging the idea that reality can ever be represented objectively without being filtered through the subjectivity and stance of the observer. They challenged the idea that the journalist does not affect the story, instead putting the journalist full square in the front of the picture. Simultaneously, they elevated subjective consciousness, theirs and others, as subjects worthy of attention.

This foregrounding of consciousness and the inclusion of the intimate, the everyday and the emotional, reflected wider social and emotional shifts. The counterculture and the social changes of the 1960s were fuelled by the questioning of traditional roles: of men and women, of races, of family position, of established authorities like church and state. Subjectivity in this context was up for interrogation. The old lofty subjects of journalism had nothing to say about these seismic shifts in consciousness whereas the inclusion of the first person, the self, meant a greater insight into this new reality. One critic describes the emergence of New Journalism as: 'it's "I" writing for an "I" time, personal writing for an age of personalism. All about us ego seems loosed in the cultural air as never before. Notions of detachment, objectivity and neutrality conflict in every sphere with a passion for uninhibited individual expression. Both one's first and last duty now belong to oneself' (Weber 1974, p. 21).

New Journalism came out of this new attention to subjectivity. Wolfe's work, says Weber (ibid., p. 21), 'has effectively portrayed this pervasive concentration on the self on the discovery of me – my life, my needs, my uniqueness'. It is, he continues, merely a 'symptom of the times – the journalist unmasking his shadow and often unburdening his soul in a period when everyone else is doing the same. If everyone nowadays is saying (as Wolfe says they are), "Look at me, I, unique...I'm new" then the New Journalism in varying degrees is merely following suit' (ibid., p. 21). Wolfe himself said the widespread discovery of the self in the 1960s and 1970s might be seen as 'one of the most extraordinary developments in American history' (cited Weber 1974, p. 21). Even for those who baulk at the introspection, the in-your-face style, the presence of literary and even fictional devices, the coverage of a reality that sometimes starts and ends with ME, it would be hard to deny the insight it has left into the period. If you want to know about this era, where could you find it better expressed than in Thompson's manic hedonism or Joan Didion's fey and drifting consciousness?

Yet along with these great strengths, New Journalism is also the place where we begin to see the first rumblings of ethical questions which have become more persistent as journalism has become ever more personal. The controversies which followed Truman Capote's *In Cold Blood* and dogged Gay Talese after *Thy Neighbor's Wife* are the first manifestations of ethical dilemmas about what responsibilities journalists have towards their real subjects when representing the characters, motivations and emotions of its subjects. Whose life is it anyway? The journalists or the real characters they describe? This of course is the issue which Janet Malcolm addressed so brilliantly in her book, *The Journalist and the Murderer* (1990). The backdrop for her book is another true life crime, the story of MacDonald, a convicted murderer who sought legal redress when a journalist with whom he co-operated to tell his story produced what he felt was a terrible misrepresentation. The struggle was over the portrayal of character, emotional life and motivation, the issue was who has the right to control the representations of living subjects.

Conventional journalism has certain conventions which protect its subjects, the conventions of standing back, not taking sides, recording accurately and refusing to project emotions or motives onto subjects. Malcolm's book addresses how, when the protective conventions of 'objective reportage' are abandoned, journalism is at risk of falsifying, projection and over-identification. She also raises something which will become much more critical, not just in journalism but all media, as the focus of interest in interviews is increasingly intimate confessional material. Hearing personal and intimate accounts creates more dependency and expectation than purely factual interviews. In this area, says Miller, 'every journalist is a confidence trickster' (1990, p. 1). Joan Didion agrees: 'writers are always selling somebody out' (1961, p. 14).

Getting Closer: Feminisation, Featurisation and the Confessional Society

4

The subjectivity of the journalist and personal, intimate issues have become steadily more visible in journalism. Arguably they have become the cornerstone of much popular contemporary journalism. Print and web journalism promote named columnists as key to their organisation's identity, recognising the pulling power of writers who provoke, entertain or mirror readers' feelings, making them feel connected to real individuals. Blogging foregrounds not just the personal voice but often intimate details of bloggers too. The status of opinion, with its reliance on personal voices and journalists with strong identities, has become ever more important, while writers' personalities are not only more visible but louder and more opinionated as well.

The previous chapter looked at New Journalism's challenge to the old journalistic illusion of itself as impartial, objective and detached. This chapter looks at some of the other important movements which have brought the subjectivity of the writer and more personal material to the fore: the feminisation of journalism; the spread of tabloid concerns and language; and the increasing preoccupation of wider culture with subjectivity and the inner life. While New Journalism was the key way in which these issues surfaced in the States, British journalism has tended to be more influenced by these three elements, converging to produce a distinctive and thoroughgoing 'featurisation' of journalism. Underlying all has been a widening of journalism's concerns and readership and a move towards including more personal material.

The 'feminisation' of journalism

One of the most important factors in bringing the personal voice to the fore has been the fallout from the 'gender-quake' of the 1970s and 1980s, which brought about changes in the style, content and priorities of journalism. As women entered journalism in greater numbers, newspaper culture changed and so did the style and stance of the writers as well as their subjects. In parallel to New Journalism's critique of professional values, women journalists began their own challenge to lofty claims of objectivity and detachment.

Women's history in journalism needs careful interpretation, but it yields insight into the trend towards increasing attention to personal and intimate issues. As with other areas such as literature, art and music, women's contributions are often overlooked, 'sometimes quite literally erased', says Conboy (2011, p. 68), 'as in Pebody's English Journalism and the Men Who Have Made It (1882) or at best marginalised within mainstream narratives'. Women are often rendered invisible or not rated like their male counterparts because men (and society) value what is produced by other men and is of interest to other men. Often because of active discrimination, women were either kept away from writing on what men regarded as the enduringly important issues of the day, or were less likely to have their work preserved.

Nevertheless scholarship has slowly rediscovered numerous women who did forge their way in journalism. *Brilliant Bylines* (Belford 1986) tells how there were actually a number of successful female journalists in America in the nineteenth century during the period when the modern press evolved. This was in spite of the fact that, unlike today, when women have independent incomes and influence household expenditure, editors and advertisers then disregarded the importance of female readership. 'Newspapers then concentrated on what men wanted to know and that meant page after page of tightly printed columns mostly about politics and business' (Belford 1986, p. 6). Consequently, the women who did get into print were often confined to the 'velvet ghetto', that is marginal or 'female' subjects. There were, of course, exceptions. Nelly Bly, discussed in Chapter 1, was valued not just for stunts like her 'Around the world in Seventy Two Days' but also for her undercover reporting. Ida Tarbell Wells became a prominent journalist who established her own newspaper in order to campaign more effectively as a black journalist on civil rights.

Women also played a crucial role in the new popular press which emerged at the end of the nineteenth century. Pulitzer at the *World* liked to use women for undercover investigations, and for the new crime story coverage pioneered by these newspapers. While men usually reported on the facts of court cases, these women often wrote side features about emotional dramas in court. Some, like Dorothy Dix, became famous but mostly these women were disparaged as 'the sob sisters' because of the sentimentality of many of their pieces (Marzolf 1977). It's interesting to see, in the overall context of this book, women's early association with emotionality, which remains a strong and controversial association in the overall history of women and journalism.

In the twentieth century, women gradually became more visible in the newsroom, but it was not a case of steady progress towards equality but rather of active discrimination and marginalisation, punctuated by occasional women breaking through (Mills 1988; Chambers et al. 2004). The lack of women columnists was symptomatic. In the 1920s and 1930s, women were still largely confined to women's pages and to what we would now call 'lifestyle' sections, although there were already several female reporters and newspaper columns were increasing in popularity (Braden 1993). Eleanor Roosevelt was one of the few women columnists; she wrote 'My Day' six days a week from 1935 to 1961. She also actively supported women journalists by organising women-only press conferences at the White House to give them an advantage. Her column was focused on domesticity but also tackled political issues.

Through the first half of the twentieth century, there were quite a few women journalists, some like Isabel Ross who was high profile; she was the first choice to cover the kidnapping of the son of famous aviator Charles Lindberg when the toddler was snatched from his bed in 1932. Newspaper writer H. L. Mencken called the kidnapping and trial, 'the biggest story since the Resurrection'. Dorothy Thompson, often called 'the first woman of American journalism', was the first female overseas correspondent; among other things, she interviewed Hitler in 1931. In 1936 Thompson began writing 'On the Record', becoming the first women to have a successful syndicated newspaper column. Thompson is an important figure for this book. She was highly partisan (the first journalist to be thrown out of Nazi Germany in 1939) and often put herself in the foreground of her coverage. 'One cannot exist today as a person – one cannot exist in full consciousness – without having to do a showdown with one's self' she said, 'without being clear in one's mind what matters and what does not matter' (cited in Quindlen 1993, p. 12). But, for 24 years between 1937 and 1961, Thompson also wrote a monthly article for the *Ladies' Home Journal*. Its topics were far removed from war and politics, focusing on gardening, children, art and other domestic and women's-interest topics. Thompson used to complain about being habitually told 'she had the brains of a man', feeling that belittled women and their interests. Her strength, she insisted, was 'altogether female'. Anna Quindlen, a key influence in the feminisation of writing, discussed later in this chapter, was a huge admirer. Thompson, she said, 'passed from nasturtiums to world events and spoke with passion' (Quindlen 1993, p. 4). Thompson, more than equal in a man's world, never turned her back on the subjects which mattered to women.

But journalism was, for the most part, an intensely male and discriminatory culture and remained so until second wave of feminism in the 1970s and 1980s. Most women who achieved national prominence before then were in 'softer' areas – columnists like Hedda Hopper and Louella Parson the queens of Hollywood gossip, Emily Post on deportment, or Dorothy Dix's advice column – all regarded as marginal to 'real journalism'. Real changes only came when increasing numbers of women entered traditionally male areas of journalism – war, politics, business, sport, commerce – and when women also began to break down the barriers and challenge hierarchies which existed between so-called men's and women's subjects.

Women's place in British journalism is less well documented but tells a similar story (Chambers et al. 2004). During the first half of the nineteenth century, women continued to contribute to magazines targeted at the fashionable, leisured female reader as they had done for most of the eighteenth century, but were excluded from the masculine world of full-time journalism on the newspapers (Conboy 2011, pp. 68–69). Journalism was one of few routes for intelligent women to pursue a career in the nineteenth century, but increasing professionalisation was very problematic for women: professional values tended to preclude women creating a vicious circle. More women therefore were found writing from home, like Margaret Oliphant and Harriet Martineau, the influential feminist writer, or contributing anonymously to pamphlets and magazines.

As in the States, there were the exceptions and pioneers: Eliza Lynn Linton, employed as Paris correspondent for the *Morning Chronicle*, was the first female full-time Fleet Street journalist, while lady Florence Dixie reported for the *Morning Post* from South Africa. Flora Shaw wrote for the *Manchester Guardian* and became Colonial editor of the *Times* and was one of the most highly regarded journalists of her time. Hulda Friedrichs, employed by Stead on the *Pall Mall Gazette*, was given important commissions and exercised considerable power on the newspaper, later taking her social reform agenda across to the influential *Westminster Gazette*. Emily Peacocke came up through the local newspaper route from the *Northern Echo* to the *Daily Express*, becoming women's page editor on the *Sunday Express*.

But when women did enter journalism, it was often through their involvement in social and political campaigns, writing in pamphlets and political magazines, so the prominence of women in journalism has tended to mirror the 'movement for political and social engagement' (Conboy 2011, p. 69). This was true at both phases of women's emancipation: the fight for suffrage and the feminist revolution which started in the late 1960s. It is interesting to note how many of the writers selected by Eleanor Mills in her collection *Cupcakes and Kalashnikovs* (2005) were not women employed full-time in newspaper offices, especially not as reporters. Instead they were women finding, or creating, alternative outlets often in the form of radical magazines.

There were some significant female journalists in the 1930s and 1940s like Rebecca West who was also a novelist and essayist. Typically, her first essay (on marriage) was in the *New Magazine*, and she became a journalist and a leading war reporter almost accidentally. Unlike Martha Gellhorn, she never sought out battlefields, nevertheless she travelled widely in Europe in the run-up to the war and its aftermath, and her powerful reporting won acclaim and many journalistic commissions. Her 1946 non-fiction book about the Balkans, Black Lamb and Grey Falcon, is still considered a masterpiece. She also covered the Nuremberg trials for the *New Yorker* and reported on apartheid in the *Sunday Times* in 1960.

The pattern in Britain, as in America, was one of a male-dominated profession, not just in terms of numbers – women were a very small minority, absent almost entirely from full-time newspaper jobs and editing – but also in terms of news values, dominated by war, foreign affairs and Westminster politics. In the post-war period, women became steadily more visible on British newspapers, not least because there was a growing recognition of the increasingly significant female readership. Through this period, the growth of consumer magazines directed at women, and often written by women, was influential as newspapers tried to emulate the success of those markets. But the women, albeit great writers, sometimes touching on social issues of the day, were more often than not confined to domestic subjects. Those whose names became well known were usually, just as in the United States, those writing lifestyle, domestic or advice columns like Marge Proops, Jean Rook and Lynda Lee Potter.

On the 'serious' newspapers, women writers gradually became more visible like the *Guardian's* Hella Pick, their UN correspondent and protégée of Alistair Cooke in early 1960s. But, even here, women were often not just confined to domestic and 'lifestyle' subjects but to women's pages too. One of the most influential newspaper figures of the twentieth century, Mary Stott, a powerful reporter and gifted editor found herself editing the *Guardian's* Women's Page. It was then known as 'Mainly for Women' and regarded as something of a ghetto, but Stott's intuitive understanding of the social changes then affecting women meant she gave space to the voices which eventually broke out of this confinement.

Everything changed in the 1960s and 1970s with the emergence of modern feminism. Feminism was just one of many 'liberation' movements during the countercultural period of the 1960s which emphasised the need for personal liberation from repressive structures and, like other movements of that era, had its roots in growing affluence and in widening education. Like other movements, women's liberation also attacked taken-for-granted traditions and authorities, specifically in this case, masculine authority. The 1960s saw women beginning to recognise and articulate their situation, creating a movement which was simultaneously political and cultural, an assault on both professional and personal relations, as women explored how they had internalised attitudes confining them to lesser roles. But, unlike other political movements, this was a movement which problematised subjectivity, seeking to explore personal feeling and behaviour as connected with wider social and political structures of oppression. This underlying philosophy gave rise to consciousness-raising groups which met to explore how female subjectivity was constructed.

Across all professions women argued that, given the same opportunities, not only were they capable of performing at the same level as men, but also that positions of professional authority, including so-called objective truth, were tainted (Kitch 1999). Journalism was no different. Feminism added weight to the push for women to win respect in traditionally male-dominated areas, with examples such as Kate Adie becoming a war correspondent for the BBC in the 1980s. But feminism also exposed how the edifice of objectivity was built on excluding and trivialising issues which affected women's status. These two battles were often fought separately. For some women what was at stake was entering the 'male' world, competing on equal terms and rendering invisible the difference between the sexes. These women disliked the idea they could be 'trivialised' by being seen as only interested in women's issues, and ghettoised on separate pages. They wanted journalism to be gender invisible. For others, the issue was about changing the valuation of the female, not denying the possibility that men and women might have interests in different issues, but instead getting recognition for those 'female' values.

Across the board, however, most feminist journalists insisted that issues and viewpoints which had routinely been ignored or looked down on by mainstream journalism should be included. Feminists called for mainstream journalism to take seriously women's viewpoints on health, fertility, childcare, work, housing, marriage and divorce. Nothing illustrates these issues more clearly than the story of the *Guardian* Women's Page, synonymous, in some minds, with the history of women's journalism through this period. From the late 1950s onwards, there were constant debates about renaming, redefining and even abolishing the pages. The main tension was precisely whether to keep a specific Women's Page in the *Guardian*, which reflected the wider tussle of feminist journalists over whether equality meant gender invisibility or could only be achieved by transforming the 'male' values which had oppressed women.

Mary Stott, mentioned earlier, is the journalist and editor inextricably associated with the *Guardian* Women's Page, not surprisingly because she was editor from 1957 to 1972. In this long stint, she was very influential not just as a columnist but because of the editorial support she gave to all sorts of campaigns and groups then bringing women's issues into wider awareness. Belonging to a slightly different generation, she was not, like later feminists, committed to the radical transformation of sex roles and family relations. However, she had an ear for the feminist rumblings which erupted so forcibly in the 1970s. Her own writing revealed this instinctive commitment. Ahead of her time, she wrote some powerful first-person pieces shedding light on the social and cultural issues affecting women. Her book, *Forgetting's No Excuse* (1975), on becoming a widow turns her evident pain at losing her husband into a plea for women to become more financially competent and independent.

The page (more precisely the group of articles designated by 'a fertility symbol') was initially called 'Mainly for Women' and through the early 1960s it was under constant review from editor Alastair Hetherington with an eye to shake it up, revise it and abolish it. When Peter Preston became Features Editor, as part of the newspaper's overall redesign in 1969, it became Women's *Guardian*. But after Stott's retirement, it was edited by various male feature editors including Brian Redhead.

In 1973, Linda Christmas became the new editor. She disliked the idea of a women's ghetto and designated the pages 'androgynous', claiming men and women were already writing on a variety of not particularly women's issues. It became the *Guardian* Miscellany and as the name implies housed many things. 'But most famously', says Gordon Taylor (1993), the *Guardian*'s historian, 'it housed Jill Tweedie', a writer whose strong sense of the value of a separate space for women more accurately represented the future of journalism.

From the point of view of this book, Jill Tweedie is a key figure. It's fair to say she came from nowhere, arriving in journalism, through a series of accidents (Tweedie 1993). Her childhood had been unhappy, spent battling a repressive, conservative father and a weak, obedient mother, parents who tried their best to force their wild rebellious, tousled haired daughter to fit their expectations of traditional womanhood. She received a pretty inadequate education and thought her only escape was through marriage but fled into an even more disastrous situation. She married an exiled Hungarian count whose views on women were as archaic as her father's, who pretty much stalked her (as we would now call it) and who ended up kidnapping her two young babies. In spite of continuously fighting get them back, she ended up not seeing them until they were in their 20s.

It was not only an extraordinary life but also a life which contained the very elements of the cocktail which exploded as feminism: rebelling against an older generation's expectations of femininity; male sexual attitudes; oppression in marriage; the struggle to control fertility; and the quest for independent income. When Tweedie finally made it back to England from Canada, where she had lived the first few years of her married life, she fell into journalism as something she had done to earn money in Canada. She found herself editing *Homes* magazine, a particularly ironic appointment given both her own distance from the idealised stereotype of the era and her subsequent journalism which attacked the edifice of male domination in the home. When she hit the *Guardian* in 1969, recruited by Hetherington from the *Telegraph*, 'she stood in relation to what had gone before as heavy metal to Handel ... more than anyone else she personified not only the liberated Guardian woman but the young, emancipated, agnostic and for most part profoundly worried clientele of both sexes'. One astonished spectator described her as 'a one woman torchlit procession' (Taylor 1993, p. 213).

From the word go, Tweedie, 'the doyenne of feminist journalists bringing the hottest of bulletins from the front line of the sex war' (ibid.) was both partisan and subjective. Although reserved about details of her life, especially the tragedy of her children, she mined other experiences. Her style, too, was the radical opposite of the remote discourse which passed for objective journalism. She wrote as she spoke and the words jumped off the page, full of colloquialisms and inner dialogue. After going on the first women's lib demo, she wrote: 'I went, unreasoningly fearful that me and my friend Ivy would be alone stomping down Regent Street, running the sneering gauntlet of Saturday shoppers. But there they were at Hyde Park Corner, all the lovely sisters, giggling and shivering, and bawdy and prim and I turned and turned again, gloating at the numbers before and behind, my motley, frost defying sex' (*The Guardian* 10 March 1971).

When Peter Preston became editor in 1975, he decided to relaunch a specific women's page, *Guardian* Women, of which Tweedie became the emblematic figure. Preston himself talks of recognising that women were a key and neglected constituency who needed to have their interests reflected in the newspaper, although the editors he appointed suspected it was an attempt to confine women to traditional interests (Preston 2010). Both of the first editors, Suzanne Lowry and Liz Forgan, immediately recognised the relevance of feminism for their own positions because they were women making their way in a difficult and unwelcoming male world of journalism. So they made the page the key space where the transformative ideology of feminism was aired. It became the home not just for Tweedie but other firebrand feminists: Erin Pizzey, Polly Toynbee and Bel Mooney (*G2* special 18 August 2007).

What was it that women brought to 'their' space? Reflecting the movement outside, it became the place where new issues and styles redefined journalism: Tweedie tackled the subject of abortion, while Pizzey put domestic violence on the agenda. The tone was different too. This was the era when *Cosmopolitan* took off, discussing sexuality and work in equal measure with equal frankness and women's journalism began to reflect this sense of female community using more personal and direct address. Eleanor Mills says 'although women can report objectivity as well as any man, what women have really brought to newspapers is a more confessional, intimate voice' (Mills and Cochrane, p. xiv). Mills and Cochrane's collection (2005) foregrounds examples of women writing like this in earlier periods, like Maddie Vegtel's 1930 account of having a baby when 40 years old, but feminism gave this writing political edge. Intimate domestic moments were often the reality of women's lives, but feminism understood how the marginalisation of these moments allowed discrimination to flourish. These new feminist writers may have been talking about subjectivity and subjective responses, but it was the opposite of introspection.

What gave this journalism such immediacy was its connection to wider political and social critiques. I started writing for the *Guardian* because the then editor, Frances Cairncross, commissioned me as young author of a new book about feminism. *Female Desire* (Coward 1984) belonged to this moment, arguing that personal desires and everyday tastes were textured by male dominance, ideas reflecting feminism's slogan 'the personal is political'. This was a sea change which validated interest in the personal and experiential and linked them to wider politics including a critique of the media's representations of women. Like the other journalism appearing on the women's page, there was an implied assault on journalism's own values. It asserted what was missing (accounts of women's lives and their concerns); it asserted why those missing issues mattered (sexual oppression was built on view which trivialised or dismissed women's concerns); and it exposed the ideologies which lay behind establishment news values including explicit pieces about women in the media, and their representations.

In a revealing piece, Tweedie (1980, p. 9) illuminates how, for feminism, exploring subjectivity was exploring social and political conditioning. She describes spotting a huge graffiti saying 'it's only me': 'A newspaper columnist, filling a weekly space with opinion and observation, thoughts and emotions, has much the same motive as that anonymous graffitist. You want to tell the world what it can do but who are you after all to tell it?' (1980, p. 9). Self-doubt, continued Tweedie, was particularly acute for the female columnist at that time – who after all would be interested in her increasingly different perceptions of life? 'Then, in the late sixties, a lot of other women who had thought "it's only me" began to think "it may be all of us" and the women's movement was born.' This time she continued, 'because I was a woman, the subject as well as the purveyor of the news, I was made acutely aware of journalistic bias in action. The whole concept of straight, "just give me the facts, ma'am" reportage fell away and revealed behind its careful smokescreen, ordinary people with peptic ulcers, childhood nightmares, job problems, sexual hang-ups, messy private lives and all the general baggage of emotion and prejudice that every human being lugs around and journalists so neatly conceal beneath the cool and apparently objective word' (ibid., p. 11).

The implied critique began to have an effect across journalism generally. Issues which previously were considered irrelevant – rape, abortion, sexual violence, childbearing – were suddenly understood as central in the experience of half the population. The appointment of Polly Toynbee as Social Affairs editor at the BBC in the 1980s showed how the old establishment and news values were shifting to include the issues and reflect the transformative gender politics of the era. There was another effect too: the gradual emergence of this more personal discourse into the body of newspapers themselves. There was a growth in lifestyle journalism as well as an expanded coverage of health but a more subjective tone begins to appear in news and opinion writing too. 'Women have already made a difference, particularly on the magazine and feature side of newspapers', said Linda Christmas (1997) 'the features content of all national daily and Sunday newspapers has increased in the last 15 years. There has been a huge increase in human interest stories'.

Across the Atlantic, Anna Quindlen, who was only the third woman to write a column for the *New York Times* op-ed pages, has provided an interesting narrative about of this process in her aptly named collection, *Thinking Out Loud, On the Personal, the Political, the Public and the Private* (1993). When she first started working as a journalist, her ambition had been to be like men and write objectively, suppressing everything personal. The reader, said Quindlen, should know no more about her than her name. 'I believed then fervently in the idea that I was meant to be hidden from the reader, a by-line without a face, a voyeur without a point of view.' Yet she was aware that who she really was, her real life and passions were not represented at all in the newspaper: 'I was hard pressed to find myself between the pages of the paper for which I worked' (Quindlen 1993, p. 15).

This wasn't simply because the women's sections, full of recipes and couture at that point, didn't reflect her interests. It was also because the main newspaper was so dull. 'There isn't much in most successful American newspapers to excite living interest, or affection, or dislike.' Such disaffection was not new. She quotes Charles Fisher approvingly, who in the 1940s had said, 'the great portion of the American press has been congealed for years in a pattern which is admirably useful and impeccably dull'. But, 40 years later in the 1980s, the situation had become 'critical': 'TV was much more dynamic and interesting. Newspapers initial response to the speed of TV was to try to give more in-depth coverage. But I believed that if newspapers were going to survive and thrive in a television age they were going to have to use their gift for words in ways they have not considered before.' What was missing, she felt, was a female perspective. She wanted to be like Thompson, 'altogether female' (1993, p. 14).

By the time Quindlen went on maternity leave, the *New York Times* had created a Living and Home section with occasional features on childrearing and so on. It had evolved enough to sign her up to write a personal column, 'Life in the 30's', which was written, she says, 'in determinedly female voice and was considerably off the usual news. While my colleagues on the op-ed pages were dissecting the Reagan administration the state of the Soviet Union…I was writing about our two young sons and the world contained within the four walls of our house' (1993, p. 16). The column was extremely successful but Quindlen dropped it after three years, vowing not to use her family again. 'I found the relentless self-exposure of "Life in the 30's" wearing, and in some ways it was a great relief, packing it in after three years, being able to be with my children without thinking, "Can I use that?" ' But, when invited back some years later onto the op-ed pages to write a supposedly conventional op-ed column, she realised the option of excluding the personal no longer existed. In words that resonate strongly with my own experience of writing op-ed columns for the *Guardian* (1995–2005), she thought it 'not only useful but illuminating for a woman writing an opinion column to bring to her work the special lens of her gender' (Quindlen 1993, p. 17). She had become aware not only of the different choices women and men were making, but also that many women felt pressurised to exclude, or deny, what were still priorities for them – families, domestic life, relationships. Women journalists began 'to admit that some of what we had once covered as hearth and home still moved us as reporters, that we believed that writing about those matters was as important for readers as the world events we had been offering them on page one' (ibid., pp. 15–17).

The irony of succeeding in the world of male journalism was to discover its limitations: 'while we began by demanding that we be allowed to mimic the ways of men, we wound up knowing we would have to change those ways. Not only because those ways were not like ours but because they simply did not work. The newspapers…were written overwhelmingly by white men for white men and so they did not reflect the communities or concerns of so many of us. If male was hard news and female was features (and that was how it broke down) the newspaper of the 21st century would clearly have to be more female' (ibid., p. 19).

Featurisation

The feminisation of journalism refers to the way in which female subjectivity and hitherto ignored, often personal, subjects of relevance to women came onto the journalistic agenda. As the 1980s progressed, these elements converged with wider cultural factors, cranking up by many degrees the focus on the personal in journalism. At the forefront of these other elements, especially in the United Kingdom, was the process often referred to as tabloidisation, that is, the spread of a tabloid journalistic agenda across journalism as a whole. This had gained traction in the 1970s, becoming a dominant trend in the 1980s, especially under the influence of Rupert Murdoch's the *Sun*. This newspaper had pioneered a brasher, more opinionated journalism which relied on more strident, subjective voices and personalities talking directly to the reader, together with a human interest – often sensationalist – driven agenda.

Many of the conventions of impersonal journalism came under attack as tabloids gained influence (Conboy 2000, 2004; Zelizer 2009). In particular, some of the old barriers between hard and soft news, objective and subjective writing, began to break down. 'Featurisation' began to affect all newspapers, broadsheets included, a development which meant two things. On the one hand personal, 'soft', subjects like health, family, emotional life and sexual relationships moved into the mainstream. On the other, more personal stories and subjective writing began to be found across newspapers more generally. As we have seen earlier in the chapter, this process was also influenced by the feminisation of news values (Christmas 1997; Keeble 2001).

In academic debates and among the journalism elite, including some broadsheet editors, tabloidisation is often used as a pejorative term implying a lowering or compromising of journalistic standards. Conboy (2000) outlining how many critics now claim tabloidisation has 'infected the whole news media market', describes their underlying view of taboidisation as the 'sensationalisation and personalisation' of the press. Referring to the way in which tabloids are often accused by these same critics of stirring up 'moral panics', that is, panics about perceived changes in social behaviour which are portrayed as threatening to social order, Conboy continues that 'as concern has spread within the elite news media, political circles and parts of the academic community, the perception of an acceleration towards tabloidisation has become a moral panic in its own right' (2011, p. 117). Yet there are few very precise definitions of what tabloidisation is. Sparks (cited in Conboy 2011, p. 117), for example, says that tabloidisation refers to 'shifts in the boundaries of journalism, shifts within the priorities of journalism, and shifts in taste in media forms' while Paletz (ibid.) says tabloidisation describes 'shifting priorities concerning content, forms of presentation, journalistic techniques and ethics'.

The model behind these descriptions is the classic British 'red top' tabloid which achieved its greatest successes in the 1980s. Tabloids, a term which originally referred to the smaller size of a newspaper, of course go back much further in the United Kingdom. Newspapers like the *Daily Express*, *Daily Herald* and *Daily Mirror* were all precursors not only in content – interested in gossip, crime and human interest stories – but also in form. But it was the *Sun*, in the late 1960s, which pioneered the distinctive format now synonymous in people's minds with the tabloids. The virtually defunct *Daily Herald* had been relaunched as the *Sun* in 1964 but this had not reversed its fortunes. Murdoch acquired it in 1969 and, this time, it burst onto the British newspaper scene, promoting itself as accessible, fun and a challenge to stuffy, boring, establishment journalism. Murdoch and his editors saw it as a deliberate attempt to recreate the anti-establishment feel that had been the hallmark of the wartime *Mirror* but which the *Mirror* had by then lost: Editor Larry Lamb (1989, p. 5) said he wanted the *Sun* to be 'strident, campaigning, working-class, entertaining but politically aware, a thorn in the flesh of the Establishment in its many guises'. The *Sun*, says Rooney (1999, p. 22), 'turned against what it saw as pompous do-gooders, planners, bureaucrats, snobs and prudes who got in the way of the fun-loving family of Sun readers'.

The *Sun* redefined not just the format but the look, using far more bold headlines and visuals. It also ran shorter stories with more attention paid to 'fun', gossip and human interest. Although still news based, the language changed, articles became shorter and there was much more use of direct address, not just in editorials but in opinion pieces and these were now scattered throughout the newspaper. Generally the tone was more emphatic and emotive, confrontational even. Murdoch, however, still saw the newspaper as having an investigative role saying 'The muckraking tradition of popular journalism is an honourable one' (cited in Conboy 2004, p. 159).

The *Sun* re-energised and expanded the tabloid market and, during the 1980s, the *Mirror* followed suit and the *Star* was launched. Tabloid newspapers really hit their stride in this decade discovering, and mining, some rich seams: on the one hand, these papers circulated news and speculation about celebrities; on the other they espoused, or perhaps actually helped create, the brash, confrontational politics of the era.

Murdoch's agenda which included challenging the power of the unions, campaigning against Europe and aggressively promoting a free market chimed closely with Thatcher's political agenda. It was also the era of Princess Diana, the 'Princess of Sales' as Greenslade (2004) dubbed her. Growing speculation about her eating habits, pregnancies, fashion and then, much more sensationally, her divorce (all conducted in the context of the gradual erosion of the deferential journalism which had previously surrounded royalty and the social and political elite) provided tabloids with an endless source of fascination and an unfolding unparalleled drama (Coward 2005).

The relationship with television was also formative for the tabloids. As television became increasingly good at breaking news, updating in real time, newspapers had to find a different role. The tabloids discovered it by bringing in more of a magazine format, providing more entertainment as well as features and opinionated commentary. Television was also important in bringing 'a new visibility and hence prominence to many aspects of human life.... Above all television has given visibility and prominence to the emotional' (Ellis 2009, p. 103). Ellis has argued that television as a medium with its close-up scrutiny has always invited an intimacy and presence not necessary to other media. But this intensified in the 1980s 'at the moment regulatory expectations were reduced which framed the definitive emergence of emotionality as they key means of understanding people and events' (Ellis ibid., p. 105).

Tabloidisation, Conboy (2005, p. 16) concludes, 'may therefore refer to an increase in news about celebrities, entertainment, lifestyle features, personal issues, an increase in sensationalism and the use of pictures and sloganized headlines as well as vulgar language, and a decrease in international news, public affairs news that includes politics, a reduction in the length of words in a story and the complexity of language and also a convergence with agendas for popular and in particular television culture'. Rooney adds 'editorial matter is presented in emotive language in easy to consume format' (2000, p. 91).

Tabloids are characterised not just by their content but by their style. Tabloid style involves the use of short, punchier sentences primarily in narrative rather than analytic mode. In addition, there is an emphasis on the personal; for instance, journalists handle major economic themes through personal stories about individual people and how they cope (Bird 2008). Turner (1999, p. 59) says tabloidisation involves a shift away from 'information based treatment of social issues and towards entertaining stories on lifestyles and celebrities and overwhelming interest in the power of the visual' and 'in news as entertaining spectacle'.

Looking at the leading 'serious' newspapers in the United Kingdom today, it's almost impossible to draw the hard-and-fast distinction between them and the red tops that was possible when the *Sun* was first launched. I use the term 'serious' instead of broadsheet because, apart from the *Daily Telegraph* and the *Sunday Times*, there are no classic broadsheet-sized newspapers now. *The Times*, under the editorship of the Murdoch, has gone tabloid sized, so has the 'I', the cheap version of the *Independent*. Although the same size as the tabloids, *The Daily Mail* has remained slightly in its own class, neither red top nor broadsheet, a middle-market tabloid carrying much more news, including international news, than the red tops but still adopting the shorter-length articles, more scattered commentary and, in particular, a large presence of feature articles. The *Guardian* and the *Observer* have adopted the Berliner format and produce a small, tabloid-sized, feature supplement.

But this is not just a question of size. Subjects or approaches to subjects which before the 1970s would not have found a place in serious broadsheets now form much of their content. All now carry a degree of celebrity news like the birth of the Beckhams' latest child and speculation such as why Victoria wanted a daughter or why was she called Harper. They also carry first-person pieces and real-life experiences; news stories introduced by feature leads and illustrated by personal stories; large feature sections; and more strident, personalised opinion pieces. Differences in subjects covered are no longer so polarised between broadsheets and tabloids. The contemporary *Guardian* and the *Mail* are, for example, surprisingly close – divided by political leaning and cultural framing maybe – but often covering similar subjects. These are sometimes human interest stories, sometimes background to celebrities in the news, and sometimes investigations into 'lifestyle' issues such as food scandals – the *Daily Mail* campaigned against 'Frankenstein foods', while in the *Guardian* (7 February 2011) Felicity Lawrence investigated the production of salad vegetables for supermarkets, an article which, incidentally, the *Daily Mail* reprinted. Peter Preston (2013) says, 'We've reached the point, for better or worse, where the old definitions of what broadsheets and tabloids should cover, are totally irrelevant'.

Will Self, in his essays Feeding Frenzy (2001, p. 5), says, disapprovingly, the *Guardian* 'is now a tabloid-broadsheet, a *Daily Mail* for the dumbed-down and deracinated, who'd rather read easy-to-swallow gobbets about Dolce & Gabbana than the kind of serious, campaigning articles that characterised the paper in its heyday'. The academics quoted earlier, who shake their heads over these developments, also take them as evidence of a decline of seriousness and a dereliction of journalism's duty to produce the informed citizen. The changes are seen as ultimately undermining democratic involvement; if readers are deprived of factual, 'objective' information, receiving instead only stories and commentary, they are no longer receiving the necessary information about what is happening in their society and politics. Fed a diet of stories, entertainment, gossip and forceful personal opinion (viewspapers instead of newspapers), the argument runs that citizens are no longer fully equipped to participate.

It is certainly the case that in a complex, mediated democracy, citizens need to be able to access full information and a range of views, but such negative views of featurisation or even tabloidisation are extreme. The ideal newspaper which seems to lurk behind these comments is like the *New York Times* that bored Quindlen so much in the 1980s, a newspaper that these days we would find tedious and unappetising with its narrow diet of serious international news and weighty political matters. It might be educational and erudite, but it is hardly inclusive. Fortunately many recognise the more positive aspects of these changes. McNair sees the changes as a positive move towards a more inclusive, even democratic journalism culture: 'less pompous, less pedagogic, less male, more human, more vivacious, more democratic' (McNair 2003, p. 50).

Defending aspects of the *Sun*, Greenslade (2003, p. 337) said it had shown 'there was an audience for softer features based material and heavily angled news in which comment and reporting were intertwined'. Smarter editors recognised what was at stake. One of the first broadsheets to go down the path towards including more features was the *Guardian*, under the editorship of Peter Preston. He became editor in 1975 and during late 1970s and 1980s continued the trend he had initiated as features editor, transforming the over serious newspaper it had once been. 'The truth – my dawning truth from 1976 – is that tabloid actually suits the current broadsheet news and feature agenda best. It's the natural way of seeking to address a segment of a readership which itself is increasingly composed of segments. It forces editors to put their judgement on the line. It establishes its own priorities, not an order of news nicked straight off the 6 o'clock news on BBC. Tabloid is much more than easy reading on the tube. It is a means to a disciplined end, a clarity of mind' (2004, p. 51).

Preston recognised the paper was 'losing readers, and needed to expand to include all the human interest etc.'. In particular, he noticed the lack of female readership. He significantly expanded the features sections, eventually introducing the tabloid *G2*. Preston created a vibrant and expanded comment and analysis section, which all broadsheets have subsequently copied. He understood that in order to keep readers and move with the times the newspaper needed to reflect the growing interest in the arts, women's issues and popular culture as well as encouraging more human interest stories.

The *Guardian*, under Preston's editorship, was also the first broadsheet to embrace the critique that emerged from feminism and elsewhere. Other newspapers followed, widening their range of subjects to include some which previously would not have met the news values criteria, including more personal and subjective material. Alan Rusbridger, responding to criticism that the flood gates opened by this have resulted in newspapers becoming too subjective, delivering soft features instead of hard news, made an interesting comparison between the *Times* now and in the 1960s. The most startling change, he said, was the increase in features. This might look like a loss of objective reportage, he says, but actually it represents the inclusion of issues previously swept under the carpet, many of which mattered a great deal to groups who had been disenfranchised by 'the men's club agenda' of the previous era: 'missing from the Times of 1968 was anything to do with the home or emotional life. There is nothing about marriage, divorce, children, schools, au pairs, depression, drinking, health, drugs, teenagers, affairs, fashion, sex, successful relationships, failing relationships, interior decor, cancer, infertility, faith, grandparents – or any of the other things that make up the texture of our non-working lives' (*The Guardian* 4 November 2000).

Feminisation and featurisation are not exactly the same thing but, as Rusbridger's and Preston's comments show, they are connected. Many of the disenfranchised subjects – home, emotions, relationships – are subjects which had and still have particular relevance for women. They are key areas where men's and women's experiences are often very different, with consequences for the public roles of men and women. For this reason, women don't just want foreign elections, rioting in Gaza and the latest fluctuations in the FTSE (Rusbridger ibid.). They want to connect to the issues of wider human interest. When newspapers recognised, and began to cater for this readership, it reinvigorated them. Until the challenge of the Internet, journalism in the 1980s and 1990s flourished as never before. With this wider agenda and more intimate voices, connecting to ordinary concerns and issues, newspapers were able to reach a far wider readership and by humanising and telling personal stories they created a new space to debate moral change.

The new intimacy

Journalism is not an isolated phenomenon and the trends we have looked at so far – the increasing importance of the personality, the push of feminism and featurisation towards more personal and intimate subjects – are both protagonists and symptoms of wider trends. Arguably one of the most significant cultural trends of the second half of the twentieth century, which escalated in the 1980s, has been a steadily growing preoccupation with subjectivity and the emotional life.

This preoccupation with self, subjectivity and identity, and especially our intimate feelings, can be witnessed in most areas of cultural life, taking many different forms. Popular culture is infused with questions about identity and subjectivity. On television, in books and on the Internet, there is a fascination with 'your story' – personal experiences, stories and reactions. Magazines and books are full of real-life stories and character-altering experiences. TV programmes explore how to improve, alter or come to terms with our characters and bodies. Family history encourages us to find out who we really are. How subjectivity is constructed, and how it affects our perceptions, are dominant themes of modern art and modern literature. This preoccupation with the self is not just with our own selves. We also want to witness others finding out who they are, what they are made of, and if they can change. Critics (Ellis 2009; Hill 2005; Bignell 2004) have exposed how television has a similar fascination with 'real people' and their experiences.

This interest is not, as it might have been in the past, with grand subjects, important people like politicians, religious leaders, the wealthy and the classic subjects of serious journalism. Autobiography and self-revelation have been democratised. Programmes like Oprah are based around the confessions of ordinary people: everyone has a story to tell now. Over the last decade, television has been dominated by 'reality TV' which 'combines ordinary people into a situation which takes them out of their everyday life either by setting them a challenge or by constructing an entirely artificial situation. What is key in this is the observation of so called real/ordinary people reacting to different situations' (Ellis 2007, p. 124). The raison d'etre of reality television is scrutinising people's lives, dilemmas and reactions to difficult situations. In programmes such as Wife Swap, real families are transported into experimental situations; in Brat Camp or Super Nanny, families expose their troubles and their attempts to get help.

According to Plummer (2001, p. 78), the start of the twentieth century was characterised by an unprecedented obsession with telling, witnessing and (importantly) recording personal life stories. It has 'become such a voluminous business that we could even start to talk of something like an "auto/biographical society": life stories are everywhere'. He locates this phenomenon within 'historical shifts brought about through accelerated industrialisation'. A number of influential sociologists (Giddens 1991; Bauman 2001; Beck and Beck-Gernsheim 2001) have suggested that a key characteristic of late modernity is this requirement for individuals to define and refine their identities reflexively. Whereas traditional society ascribed people roles in which they often remained for life, late modernity is premised on people finding, creating or exploring subjectivity, their own and others. The increasing interest in personal revelations, memoirs and intimate revelations is part of this exploration of subjectivities which are no longer fixed but up for grabs. Self-revelation and scrutiny of other's intimacies are about witnessing others create themselves and respond to ethical dilemmas. What is striking is that identity is seen not as something fixed and given but fluid and changeable. Many autobiographical or confessional accounts are dominated by narratives of transformation, describing journeys from one state of being to another, often journeys of self-discovery or struggles to triumphant changes. 'What lies at the heart of this...is the idea that a highly individuated, self-conscious and unstable identity is replacing the old, stable, unitary self of traditional communities.' The new selves 'are "constructed" through shifts and changes in the modern world, and partly create a new sense of permanent identity crisis'(Plummer 2001, p. 83).

The roots of this focus on identity and emotions lie in the breakdown of traditional sources of authority. Earlier chapters of this book have explored some of this: the explosion of the counterculture in the 1960s; feminism's challenge to male dominance; the growth of consumerism; and the increasingly sceptical attitude towards the establishment. These have been hugely important elements in creating more equitable, democratic societies with less readiness to blindly follow the moral strictures of traditional society. But this breakdown of traditional sources of authority also created uncertainty and insecurity. How do you behave in a context where there are no longer sources of authority telling you what to do? What are the rules for sexual relationships, for example? How should you parent your children? How should you face illness and even death?

Into this vacuum comes the scrutiny of other people and their behaviour where great value is placed on having lived through an actual experience. We want to hear from people who have experienced things directly, hence the media's fascination with real lives and real experiences. You could even say we fetishise reality since far greater value is put on descriptions given by people who have lived through experiences than scenarios imagined in fiction, or reports based on research and canvassed opinion as in conventional feature writing. Interest in the personal arises in this context of the need for real-life stories to witness by which we can measure ourselves. It is as if in a culture which is no longer under strict moral instructions from traditional authorities (the church, parents, the state) we are asking not how should we react, but how would we react? (Coward 2009).

The move towards more intimate personal material clearly has deep cultural roots and cannot just be dismissed as introspection and dumbing down. But that does not mean either that there are no problems with this kind of journalism, nor that their forms and ethics cannot be submitted to scrutiny.

5 Confessional Journalism

Introduction

Open any newspaper, especially at the weekend, and you will encounter a flood of first-person writing, usually about 'real-life experiences', often focusing on intimate details of writers' personal and emotional lives. Confessional journalism is everywhere, whether it's the first-person accounts at the heart of much contemporary feature writing, 'one-off' real-life stories, journalists revealing personal experiences or personal columns following writers' daily lives. Whatever form it takes, few subjects are off-limits nor, given typical articles like 'I lost my sex drive with chemo', are there many inhibitions. Thirty years ago such writing was non-existent, especially in serious newspapers. Now, its presence across so many journalistic outlets, whether conventional media or online, is one of the most striking aspects of contemporary journalism. In many ways, 'confessional journalism' is the apotheosis of the trends I have been exploring in this book.

What is confessional writing?

Personal writing has, as we have seen, a long history in journalism and has had a presence, and a function, within the most conventional journalistic outlets. In the previous chapter, I showed how mainstream journalism came to include more personal, emotional material which had previously been marginalised but which was important both to the groups affected by the issues and to society more widely. But the kind of confessional journalism now appearing is something qualitatively different; there has been a step change in the ever more intimate and explicit content as well as the sheer quantity.

While many forms of journalism are declining, confessional writing is flourishing. Editors are hungry for real-life true stories and direct experiences, the more extreme the better: 'Do you have a personal story about the break-up or survival of a marriage?' asks the *Daily Telegraph*'s Features Department (20 February 2006). Sometimes these are submitted by readers, but often a journalist will be dispatched to craft interviews into continuous first person, 'as told to', pieces; there are even agencies devoted to finding real-life stories to supply to magazines and feature writers. Newspaper sections like the *Sunday Times*' 'News Review', the *Guardian*'s 'Family' supplement and Femail in the *Daily Mail* are full of this kind of writing while the phenomenal success of the *Daily Mail*'s website lies in the importance it gives to real-life, intimate stories. As the *Telegraph* editor's appeal indicates, the preferred stories are about intimate, domestic material, particularly crises around relationships, the body, illness, misfortune and death.

While the public is a great source for one-off real-life stories, many journalists themselves now also produce this material, not just feature writers, but news writers or even war correspondents too. Such journalists would, in the past, have eschewed this as undermining their credibility. Now even journalists most closely associated with so-called impersonal, objective journalism dabble in the genre. Alan Rusbridger, editor of the *Guardian*, has written about his father's death (*The Guardian* 1 July 2005), while the BBC's defence correspondent Frank Gardner has written not just an account of being critically injured when reporting but also his life story up to, and after, this catastrophic event (Gardner 2009).

Such is the appetite for personal material that some journalists now make a living from it, either writing ongoing columns about their daily lives, or plundering their experiences at regular intervals. Journalist Tim Lott has written about his mother's suicide, his depression, his relationship with his brother, and, recently, a domestic column about fatherhood in the *Guardian*'s Family section. Tanya Gold similarly mines her own life; 'Why do my exs hate me?' she asks in a feature for the *Guardian* weekend (19 July 2008), where she hounds past boyfriends until they tell her. There are freelancers, like Anna Pasternak, whose writing in the *Daily Mail* is often personal on subjects like her divorce, or therapy. On the death of her mother, she wrote, 'The call that I had dreaded my entire adult life came, a bolt out of the blue', reducing her to 'a free fall of panic and sobbing uncontrollably' (17 March 2012).

Defining confessional writing is not straightforward since it takes many forms. It includes a writer like Will Self describing his illness from a rare blood disorder in wry reflexive prose, as well as Rachel Cusk's literary introspection about becoming a mother and her subsequent painful divorce or Allison Pearson's rather more matter-of-fact account of her struggle with depression. It can be an 'ordinary' person with a (usually) rather out-of-the-ordinary experience, like 'My Grandmother delivered my baby' (*The Guardian* November 2012); an extraordinary person talking about ordinary experiences, like a celebrity on their daily life; or journalists themselves writing about their own experiences including personal columns by regular writers charting their personal lives, ranging from problems like cancer to Tim Dowling's minor day-to-day irritations in the *Guardian Weekend* magazine.

In spite of this variety, there are shared characteristics in form and function which justify treating them as a distinct genre: confessional writing. The personal voice is what matters here, a personal voice about real personal experience. Confessional writing is interested primarily in emotions, and feelings. Even those which could just be good stories in their own right are invariably focused on the protagonists' reactions. Typically, the content of these articles deals with difficult, even harrowing, situations and how the writer coped with them: 'Five weeks ago I found out I had cancer', starts a typical article (Laura Smith *Stylist* October 2011) or 'I had to give my baby up for adoption' (Angela Patrick *The Guardian* 17 March 2012). Extreme is interesting but extreme suffering is better. Even the more mundane domestic columns are infected by this taste for not quite misery but at least a life full of irritations and misfortunes.

All this different writing is united by an intimate, confiding and self-exposing voice. The writer addresses the reader as if confiding emotionally intimate details directly to another individual. This writing tends to provoke powerful engagement with readers who write in offering sympathy, advice and criticisms, a key reason for their popularity with editors. Becky Gardiner, and her co-editor Sally Weale, commissioned Julie Myerson's 'Living with Teenagers' and had initial doubts given the intimate nature of some of the material. But always 'offsetting any ambivalence we felt, was the extraordinary response from readers'. Although they received complaints, 'we received many, many more letters from readers for whom the columns resonated. Thank you, they said, for showing me I am not alone' (*The Guardian* 10 March 2009).

This writing is also more specifically 'confessional'. Confessional is a word which comes from the religious practice of the confession where a congregation member can seek a personal and private encounter with a priest to 'confess' to their 'sins' and failings. It's also a word which has been appropriated by therapy to describe the practice by which an individual can speak – again in private – with another individual about matters weighing on, if not their conscience, at least their psyche. This writing is confessional in both those senses. Writers 'own up' to aspects of behaviour or feelings which are intimate, private or personal, often speaking about things which are painful, and shameful, to admit. Much of this writing is confessional in the therapeutic sense also, admitting difficult feelings to help you feel less burdened by them.

There is a paradox, however. The main focus of this writing is subjective experience and perceptions, but this journalism is also supposed to be truthful, based on real events. The sections in which they appear often highlight this: they are 'True Stories', 'Real Lives' and 'First Person Experience'. Under these headlines are the first-person accounts of emotional difficulties, like Sophie McKimm on how 'her grandmother has fallen in love with a 25-year-old man from the Gambia' (*The Guardian* 23 April 2007) or 'Domestic violence destroyed my family' (*The Guardian* 21 April 2007)

As discussed in the previous chapter, this hunger to witness real lives is not confined to journalism. The same fascination with real experiences, especially difficult ones, and emotional reactions is present on television, in books and on the Internet. In book publishing, few genres have been as successful recently as 'misery memoirs', 'true stories' of harrowing childhoods, like barrister Constance Briscoe's memoir *Ugly* (2006). The Internet feeds this fascination with personal blogs while on Facebook people 'update' intimate details of their lives not only to friends but also to strangers. Real-life confessions are so much part of Internet experience that Andrew Keen (2007) has dubbed much Internet content 'digital narcissism'.

The impulse to witness how people respond to difficult life events may be widespread, but it has an inherent problem, that of authenticity. Across all different discourses promoting autobiographical revelations by real people, falls the possibility of fakery. How can we know these self-revelations are true? The answer is: we can't, something which has caused book publishers considerable embarrassment recently. Both Constance Briscoe's *Ugly* and Kathy O' Beirne's *Don't Ever Tell* (2006), about abusive childhoods, have been disputed by their families. Briscoe's sister described her as 'devious and dangerous' (cited in *The Guardian* 12 January 2008). Meanwhile, James Frey's *A Million Little Pieces* (2003) told of drug addiction, criminality, imprisonment and a struggle to personal redemption. It was Oprah's book choice and sold millions until exposed as a fake by a group of investigative journalists. Frey claimed he was arrested when out of his head on crack and alcohol. He claimed he hit a police officer with his car, reacted violently to arrest, was charged with assault with a deadly weapon and ended up with an 87-day jail sentence. The reporters found the policeman who revealed Frey had been issued with two traffic tickets, one for driving under the influence of alcohol and one for driving without a licence, and had received a misdemeanour criminal summons for having an open bottle of beer in his vehicle. He had been in police custody a mere five hours.

There are many more examples of what journalist Catherine Bennett has called this 'flourishing sub-genre: miserable true-life memoirs of questionable or contested veracity' (*The Observer* 9 March 2008). The question of authenticity stalks all this autobiographical outpouring as its shadow since only 'authenticity', 'truthfulness' or an ability to 'reconstruct the facts' make these accounts autobiography rather than fiction. Authenticity is therefore the holy grail of a culture needing to see how real people react to real difficulties. Yet in most of the places where these real-life tales are told – in magazines, on Jerry Springer, on reality TV – authenticity can't be guaranteed.

The need for authenticity gives journalism a specific role in this wider cultural impulse (Coward 2009). Journalism at its best is associated with giving us facts, not making things up. Journalism brings an aura of authenticity, which is why it has proved a surprisingly compatible milieu for personal confessions. Journalists are meant to be truthful and operate within a profession which values veracity more highly than almost anything else. This is not meant to suggest that the press is a model of probity. Given recent press scandals in the United Kingdom, which led to and have been given a thorough airing by the Leveson Inquiry (2011), it would be deluded to suggest the British press is committed always to telling the truth. Yet it is noteworthy that many of the scandals which have been explored by Leveson (phone tapping, bribery, entrapment) are scandals of unethical practices aimed at uncovering a story and not, by and large, scandals of fakery. Indeed the scandals are associated with finding out about the intimate private real lives of people.

In a culture hungry for real experiences, and intimate self-revelation, journalism's professional values appear to guarantee authenticity. An article by Martin Townsend, a well-respected *Guardian* writer, shows how these values are called into play. His article 'I lived with and around my manic depressive father' opens by establishing the professional values of journalism; 'As a journalist and editor for nearly 30 years, I have come across countless depressing stories about mental illness' (*The Observer* 16 April 2007). Newspapers elicit expectations of truthfulness which puts them in a prime position to carry this kind of writing while established journalists become particularly desirable to do it. War correspondent, Ben Brown, recently wrote a telling piece of autobiographical journalism about war reporting. The piece highlights and reinforces journalism's claims for truthfulness based on accurate witnessing while at the same time embodying the trend towards a much more personal type of writing. This is a confessional piece by an old-school 'detached' journalist, but what Brown 'confesses' to is his detachment, his lack of emotions, during traumatic events he witnessed (*Mail* on Sunday 7 June 2009). Thus the piece reinforces conventional journalistic values while simultaneously offering up a corrective, a confession of feelings: ironically in this case, a lack of feelings. The mutual dependency of confessional journalism and conventional journalism peeps through here. Authenticity – facticity – is no longer enough, the public wants to know the person and see their reactions to events but this confessional journalism needs reciprocal authentication. In a culture hungry for real experiences, for personal intimate self-revelation, journalism's professional values appear to guarantee authenticity.

By giving confessional writing a home, journalism not only locks into dominant cultural trends but has a key position in authenticating confessions. But, as we will see, journalism may 'authenticate' pieces of confessional writing, but that doesn't make them 'true'. Confessional writing still has its conventions. It may be straight from the heart but, inevitably, it also conforms to norms and expectations about what these stories should contain and how they should be told. Everyone who sets out to write in this form has other examples in the back of their mind, just like every reporter trying to be objective has the work of 'objective' journalists who have gone before and who they have to live up to.

Love it or loathe it: Controversies

Confessional journalism divides critics and journalists on its very existence. The trend has its keen supporters like Tanya Gold, who has written 'about my recovery from alcoholism, my eating disorder and my ex-boyfriends'. 'Confessional journalism', she says, 'can make people realise that they are not alone and that their newspaper sees them'. It has produced much 'superb newspaper writing in the last 20 years'. 'What, after all, is the job of the confessional columnist? To provoke, to entertain, to normalise taboo topics; often to shock, occasionally to overstep the mark' (*The Guardian* 4 May 2009). This writing is therapeutic, many claim, not just for the readers who see their problems reflected in print but for the writers themselves. 'I think every time I [write about myself]

I'm providing a service', says journalist Christa d' Souza. 'I'm providing a service to myself...because it's therapeutic. Most people are supposed to write it down and then crumple it into a ball and throw it away; we don't, it just happens that it's printed' (*The Guardian* 25 February 2012).

But it has passionate critics too for whom this writing represents everything wrong with contemporary journalism. As long ago as the 1970s, Tom Wolfe aimed a brilliant swipe at personal columns (which appeared earlier in America) as unredeemably trivial and 'pathetic'. After a few weeks, he says, the writers 'start to dry up. You can see the poor bastards floundering and gasping. They're dying of thirst. They're out of material. They start writing about funny things that happened around the house the other day. Homey one liners that the Better half or the Avon lady got off, or some fascinating book or article that got them thinking, or else something they saw on the TV...anytime you see a columnist trying to squeeze material out of his house, articles, books or the television set, you've got a starving soul on your hands. You should send him a basket' (Wolfe 1973, p. 25). As columns have become increasingly personal, such criticisms have intensified. Journalism, say these critics, ought to be about the outside world and external affairs, not introspective and narcissistic rambling. This writing, they say, is catering for a dumbed down, depoliticised readership, no longer interested in the wider world, only voyeuristically titillated by extreme stories of individuals hit by misfortune.

Confessional journalism is controversial in content too, often provoking huge amounts of commentary, 'twitter storms' and even scandals about their subject matter. In an article headed 'There are downsides to looking this pretty', Samantha Brick wrote about 'why women hate her' for being 'too pretty' (*The Daily Mail* 5 April 2012). Her article told how men she didn't know had sent champagne across to her table in restaurants, or spontaneously paid for her rail ticket after standing behind her in a queue, all because of her prettiness. Women, by contrast, she claimed couldn't cope and were jealous and often spiteful to her. The article was followed by over 5000 posts, spoof articles and endless comments in newspaper columns and radio phone-ins. Brick herself appeared on breakfast shows and even her husband was interviewed about living with this paragon.

Brick's self-absorption is however a pale imitation of the real 'queen of confessional journalism', as columnist Liz Jones was labelled in an interview with Rachel Cooke for the *Observer* (2 August 2009). Jones can barely press the send button on her articles before another storm starts. Although ostensibly she sometimes writes about other subjects – from child labour, through expectations on girl models to retired racehorse sanctuaries, she invariably includes intimate material about herself. Frequently her articles include some shocking revelation about her life, whether it's the extremes of her anorexia, her obsessive compulsive disorder, some disappointing sexual encounter or her scathing views on people she knows. In recent *Daily Mail* articles, Jones has provoked outrage for her 'brutally honest account' of her £15,000-pound facelift (17 June 2011), shortly after declaring she was so broke she couldn't even afford to feed her cats, for writing about how she had 'harvested' sperm from a husband unwilling to procreate with her (her 'most shocking confession yet' 3 November 2011) and for writing about famine in Somalia ('Liz Jones in a Somalian refugee camp' 17 August 2011), a mere three months after penning 'My shoulders are so bony I look ill. But I'd still rather be dead than fat' (16 May 2011). The Internet exploded with comments, spoofs and blogs but when so much depends on newspapers/websites attracting 'visitor numbers' and other media attention, editors would not view this controversy as unwelcome.

Jones started as a fashion journalist and became editor of *Marie Claire* (1999–2001). However, it was her confessional journalism, in particular her diary about her disastrous marriage to Nirpal Dhaliwal, which shot her to prominence and has made her the highest paid female journalist in the United Kingdom. Her saga of her marriage in the *Guardian* provoked such strong public responses that the *Daily Mail* soon poached her. For most of the seven years of her relationship she gave detailed weekly updates. Readers, said Rebecca Seal (*The Observer* 13 May 2007), knew that 'Nirpal has terrible wind and likes to be called "the boss" in bed, that Liz lied about her age when they met and possibly strong-armed him into marriage, is insanely neurotic around the house and hates the fridge to be empty of San Pellegrino. Now they are divorcing and loudly sharing their grief in our newspapers, too.' Jones' diary has continued after the divorce, charting her disastrous move to the country, her isolation and an affair with a mysterious rock star who many readers believe is a fictional creation. She provokes 'loving and loathing in equal measures', says Tanya Gold (*The Guardian* 4 May 2009) but is often the first item readers go to.

Controversies often extend beyond what writers say about them and include what they say about others. At the invitation of a quick-thinking editor, Jones' husband was invited to retaliate in the *Evening Standard*. Some of the neighbours she has insulted in Somerset as being 'toothless', hostile and dirty have retaliated in print too. Jones invariably uses her column to express her bewilderment at why friends, acquaintances, ex-partners and neighbours object to becoming copy fodder. But many of the subjects of these columns are not professional or powerful and their objections and reactions such as cold shouldering Jones when they meet, recall the issues raised by the scandal which erupted when Julie Myerson wrote about her teenage son (discussed in the Introduction to this book). Most confessional writers have at some time or another run up against members of the public, other journalists, or even the subjects of the articles, protesting about the invasion of theirs and others' private lives, a subject I will return to.

These controversies are personal for me. My own journalism, which started as a feature writer and evolved into writing social and political commentary on the op-ed pages, has been increasingly personal and revelatory. My personal column 'Living with Mother' (*The Guardian* 2006–2008) was about my mother's dementia and included material about my partner and children and my wider family as well as describing intimate things affecting my mother. I never doubted the importance of tackling this subject in a very personal way. As the number of people affected by dementia increases, so does the 'problem' of how we care for them. Caring for my mother was having a huge impact on my life, as dramatic as the impact of becoming a parent, yet there was very little written about it and nothing which cast light on this hugely significant part of my life. I had no doubts that an involving personal narrative about a real situation, humanising the interaction with professionals and services, was not just journalism I'd be inclined to defend, but was journalism I considered important.

I also experienced directly the claims about the therapeutic nature of this kind of writing, both for myself and for the readers. Confessional columns attract huge 'post bags' – email responses and comments online – and mine was no exception. I received many comments from readers who felt helped by reading about others dealing with similar issues. Reciprocally, I felt reassured to hear from people with similar stories and similar reactions. Christa d'Souza says that writers who want to share everything are doing a service. 'It's helpful for other people who may be going through whatever it is – breast cancer, surgery, depression. It's so wonderful reading other people's stories. Some people want to share every aspect of their lives' (*The Guardian* 25 February 2012).

Nor did confessional journalism feel like a drastic departure for me. As discussed earlier, I was one of the many women writers who challenged the old hierarchy of what were deemed 'important' subjects. To include marginalised subjects and personal experience was not only a way of foregrounding what mattered to women, but it was also a way of humanising the news, making it possible to care about the human being affected by news. These were democratising impulses. Yasmin Alibhai-Brown, who has written powerfully on intimate subjects such as the disintegration of her first marriage and death of her mother, has spoken (in conversation 2007) about the wider significance of this kind of emotional journalism arguing these subjects are important not just for feminist reasons but also because they are what makes us human: journalism which has no space for this excludes the most important part of our being. 'Newspapers should tell the story of our times', says Russell Frank (2004, p. 51) endorsing this point, 'Public life is part of that story, so is private life'. Alibhai-Brown has also (ibid. 2007) talked of how this journalism reflects the lifting of repression, airing subjects previously hidden as too painful or shameful: cancer, grief, domestic violence, sexual inhibitions, eating disorders and family life itself. Now, by contrast, experiences which shape our lives need no longer be hidden but faced, shared and understood.

These are the ideas and influences which shaped my own journalism. Yet there have been many moments when I have encountered dilemmas and had doubts and hesitations, sometimes over the implications for others of my own journalism (the ethics) and sometimes over the content of pieces by other writers. For example, where exactly was the line that divided my sense of justification about writing of my mother's physical indignities while feeling horrified when reading Liz Jones' description of harvesting her lover's sperm from a used condom in order to conceive a baby he didn't want?

Yvonne Roberts who recognises, applauds and has participated in the feminist redefining of journalism, has also expressed reservations about the directions confessional journalism is now taking: 'Most journalists have written two or three features in their careers that are personal: often to campaign, to try to make a difference to the failing status quo. The personal story isn't the star of the show, it is the human connection to a system that needs change, for example, the treatment of dementia or cancer or mental illness' (*The Guardian* 25 February 2012). This kind of writing is enormously valuable. But, she continues, 'Personal experience, first heavily employed by male writers, is now a major part of the depoliticised end of women's writing and occurs on an unremitting basis as the "me" in "media" colonises ever larger continents of journalism. Narcissism rules; enlightenment suffers' (ibid.). According to Roberts, writing, which once had a role in highlighting social issues, has now become an introspective end in itself with particular implications for women writers (a theme to which this chapter will return).

Clearly, confessional journalism provokes strong feelings. But whether it is dismissed or defended, it is rarely deconstructed to reveal its conventions, its pitfalls and ethical dilemmas. Yet no less than with so-called objective journalism, subjective journalism is a construction, relying on definite conventions with definite consequences for how the world is represented and can have negative consequences for both journalism and journalists themselves. The remainder of this chapter examines the conventions, forms and functions, of this kind of writing as well as its context and ethical consequences.

Conventions and consequences

Many of confessional journalism's characteristics and conventions were first apparent in the personal 'daily life' column. In America, these were known as the 'local' columnists (Riley 1993). In the United Kingdom, such columns were mainly found in magazines or women's pages, only moving into weekend and features sections in the 1990s. Russell Frank is an astute analyst of this form. 'The fundamental contradiction at newspapers is that they must report the truth or lose credibility while they must also tell stories or lose readability. Over-rating readability ... can lead to sensationalism, subjectivity, fabrication, composite characters and reconstructions. Overrating credibility (or underrating readability) results in a boring newspaper' (2004, p. 47). Frank claims, the 'tension between truth-telling and story-telling is particularly exquisite just now' because newspapers are struggling to find 'what they can offer that electronic media cannot'. Part of the answer, he says, 'appears to be story-telling', in particular in the form of the personal column because it also allows the reader to know a writer. The personal columnist presents the newspaper's more human face (quite literally when the photo accompanies the column), a point of identification between the Olympian heights of the impersonal newscaster and the reader's humdrum lives.

Frank, who has written such a column himself for the *Centre Daily Times*, points out that while the readership is keen to witness intimate details of another's life and to have their own concerns reflected, they can also be antagonised and alienated if the writer appears to be too grand or successful. Consequently, personal columnists are under contradictory impulses: on the one hand such writers need quite an inflated sense of the importance or significance of their own lives to tell the world all its details. People seeing your photo and knowing about your life is 'quite an ego trip', he says, 'the columnist is inordinately vain. Smaller than life in his mug shot, he is bigger in his ego' (2004, p. 52). But, he continues, 'the problem is no-one likes a show off. Nobody wants to hear about your fabulous vacation, your over achieving children or your amazing carpentry. And so like the coyote who burns his own anus and eats his intestines, the personal columnist cuts himself down to size' (ibid.). In the United Kingdom, *Times* columnist Mary Ann Seighart's reputation was temporarily damaged when she failed to observe this convention, instead making frequent references to her talented daughters. The satirical magazine *Private Eye* created a fictional simulacrum called Mary Anne Bighead whose children were called 'Brainella' and 'Intelligencia'.

Pointing to a key element in the successful confessional column, Frank describes how the central persona of the column is frequently an unthreatening, helpless sap. Riley noticed the same: 'a good number of self-directed columns are also self-effacing' (Riley 1993, p. xvi). Frank provides some delightful examples of this rhetorical strategy, like one columnist who says the editor, 'whose crack pot idea it was to hire me', must share 'the credit and the blame' for his columns or the travel columnist who describes himself as 'a cowardly world traveller' (Frank 2004, p. 52). Incompetence, says Frank, is a recurrent theme, especially with household goods, as is the sensible or competent spouse or child created as the foil for the incompetent columnists. 'One may not write about one's trip to paradise unless things go seriously awry' (ibid.). 'The worse the experience the better the column' is something of an undercurrent in confessional columns.

It would be hard to imagine a better example of this than Tim Dowling's weekly column for the *Guardian* magazine. Each week a carefully crafted story reveals Dowling as incompetent, the butt of his wife's scorn and the helpless sap whose children run rings around him. His domestic life is presented as one of endless small irritations and minor disasters. Generically speaking, it is closest to a sitcom: predictable set characters who do not change, grow up, or evolve but endlessly repeat their predictable actions. Frank highlights the artifice of these columns, 'If the narrator in my column looks a bit like me that's because he is my stunt double, the real me could not survive all the mishaps and the humiliations to which my narrator is subjected. Russell Frank, the writer of the column and the "I" who inhabits the column are not the same person.' The column, Frank says, 'is portrait of the artist. Like all tellers of true stories the personal columnist dips into the stream of experience only a bucket at a time. The me nobody knows spends an inordinate amount of time engaged in un-story like pursuits even when I am awake, these readers do not hear about.... Like its big siblings the autobiography, the memoir and the personal essay, every personal column is a version, a representation, a construction a send up. It is not the reader's life laid bare. It is not even a mirror image but experience filtered through memory and imagination and shaped into anecdote' (ibid., p. 53).

This feels familiar. In my column, while remaining factually accurate, I elided occasions and left a lot out. There are members of my family who didn't want me to write the column so I used circumlocutions to avoid mentioning them. I cherry picked what went in and what was left out. I created voices and personalities who were strong enough to carry a 'story'. The 'I' in the story was a parallel self, truthful to the issues and difficulties surrounding caring for someone with dementia and truthful about my reactions, but certainly not without artifice. Philip Roth once wrote, 'to suggest my writing is autobiographical is not only to slight the suppositional nature of my writing but also to slight the art that goes into making it seem autobiographical' (cited in Benn *The Guardian* 3 April 2008)

John Diamond foregrounded this in a particularly dramatic column when he went public with his cancer diagnosis (*The Times* 12 April 1997). In passing his words gave a devastatingly astute account of the rhetorical devices of the confessional journalist. 'The me you meet here', he said, referring to his pre-diagnosis column, 'isn't the real me. He looks much the same as the real me, has the same number of wives and children, combines wit and witlessness in roughly the same proportions, has lived much the same life in many of the same places, but you will understand that if each week I were to deliver to you my life unpasteurised and absolutely as I experience it then that life would be unliveable.... The me you see here is a sort of parallel me, picking and choosing the details which will best make the point, changing names or job titles out of a sense of propriety or social cowardice, baring a virtual soul and taking risks only where no risk really exists'.

'Until last week', he added. Diamond wrote these dramatic words because he had just been diagnosed with cancer. 'What do you know?' he continued, 'I had cancer all along. And have it still. The hubris-hating gods, it seems, read The Times too.' Diamond ponders the dilemmas: 'So here's my problem. Well, not my real problem, which is that I have cancer and may expire before the date printed on the packet, but my columnar problem.' Should he write about cancer in a 'jaunty week-end column'? Can he continue to be jaunty if the treatment makes him sick? Should he? If he recovers, won't he sound 'smugger than ever'? 'Normally I try to address any qualms I have about what I'm about to write before I sit down to write it. This time, I'm sorry, I can't. There you are: the truth, at last.'

It seems that the desire to witness is very much a desire to witness weakness and, if not quite failure, then problems, disappointments, hardship and in some cases extreme suffering. At the 'jaunty' end, the personal columnist is often wryly amused by his or her general uselessness; at the serious end, the confessional writer is often tortured. This pressure towards emotional difficulties and weaknesses has, as Roberts suggested (*The Guardian* 25 February 2012), particular implications for women especially as the appetite has grown for a more intimate, self-exposing, raw confessional journalism.

There are of course male domestic columnists like Tim Dowling mentioned earlier and Chris Cleave who wrote 'Down with the Kids' about fatherhood in the *Guardian* (2008–2010). Indeed, arguably the first confessional column in a British newspaper was written by a man, William Leith, who according to Tim Adams (*The Observer* July 2005) 'was perhaps some years ahead of his time'. Before television and magazines were filled with the intimate personal confessions of people you did not know, claimed Adams, Leith 'had written a column for the Independent on Sunday of such startling introspection that he had become a sort of poster boy for a new kind of journalism. At The Observer, he started as he meant to go on: one of his earliest pieces for this paper was a 6000-word article on masturbation, dwelling principally on his own inevitably tortured history with the subject.... Before it became routine, he made all of his readers rubber-neckers, slowing down for a few moments to survey the quiet damage of the writer's days.'

However, many of the journalists working in this genre are women, since domesticity and emotionality have strong female associations and it is around women that the more problematic aspects of these conventions surface. At the more lightweight end, several high-profile female columnists exploit the 'hopeless' persona offering themselves up as prone to failure – at dieting, relationships, social occasions. Columnist Julie Birchill led the way in the 1990s. She combined opinionated pieces with personal domestic detail but in spite of her abrasive, political self-confidence, the persona she created was surprisingly unthreatening, prone to spending long periods on her sofa, watching a lot of television. Columnists like Zoe Williams, Lucy Mangan and the Tanya Gold (all writing in the *Guardian*) have formed themselves in this likeness, all sofa sisters. These are mainly humorous writers, foregrounding their failures and personal inadequacies, like Tanya Gold writing about her disastrous attempt to camp at Glastonbury and their columns are self-exposing, rather than self-mutilating. But it's concerning when so many of the leading female columnists, driven by the aesthetic convention of the unthreatening narrator, cast themselves as hopeless and lacking in self-discipline. Far from opening up domestic and emotional life to scrutiny, it is closing it down with a potentially humiliating stereotype of female incompetence and lack of self-control.

When it comes to the raw confessionals – an area where women's writing definitely predominates – the helpless woman stereotype can give way to women as psychologically disturbed and damaged. Confessional journalism invariably focuses on problems, failures and disasters like broken relationships, problems with children, traumatic sexual experiences, sexual problems, divorces and stalking. Freelance journalist Jill Parkin (*The Guardian* 27 April 2009) argues this has particular implications for women. She describes articles in which female journalists expose weaknesses and failures, especially in relation to body image and body loathing, as 'fem-humiliation' and argues that there is an enormous appetite among commissioning editors for this material: 'right now it's just about the best-paid thing there is because the appetite for fem-humiliation among commissioning editors is insatiable'. She describes how one female journalist became known as the 'fat writer': 'She's told us how she wakes up with chocolate all over her bed from gorging herself the night before; we've heard how in desperation she took a weight-loss drug that gets rid of fat through defecating; and we have had – recently running in The Daily Mail – a weight loss contest between her and another overweight woman journalist. These are not things that men are ever asked to do. Body hatred is the main staple of women's confessionals at the moment.'

Parkin describes how she has experienced pressure to produce this kind of copy, claiming the recession has made it more difficult for freelancers to get commissions but 'not if you can find something weird or shameful about yourself to write up.... Editors no longer want my shorthand or my interviewing skills, or even my way with words. They want my body and soul, two things I'm not used to hawking'. She is not alone in noticing the trend: numerous women feature writers report experiencing pressure towards 'emotional striptease'. An ex-editor of a leading women's consumer magazine, now freelancing for national newspapers, who preferred to remain anonymous, agrees, speaking of pressures she now experiences from feature editors to include intimate experiences (interview with author 20 July 2009). These are pressures which as an editor she would never have put on writers. Feature writers have noticed that editors are particularly keen to see articles which reveal shortcomings and personal difficulties: they often feel pressurised to come up with more extreme experiences or feelings. Rachel Johnson, who for many years wrote the 'Mummy Diaries' in the *Daily Telegraph*, has said 'You are under an immense pressure from your editor to put in as much personal material as possible, especially if they know what your specific weaknesses are' (cited in Matthew Bell 'Keep it the family' *The Independent* 15 March 2009).

Again, it is Liz Jones who both embodies and raises the bar of these trends. In one classic passage, she complains about a 'dress therapist' using the opportunity to do what she does best: self-flagellate and expose some really rather disturbed mental states. 'She missed that I am borderline anorexic, have body dysmorphic disorder, fear ageing, men and sex, that I am in awe of clothes rather than know how to enjoy them, and that I spend way too much money. She should have deduced, as a therapist who claims to use only clothes to make her diagnosis, that I am divorced, that I hate my body, am hugely stressed, and – oh! – that I'm broke!' (*The Daily Mail* 25 April 2012). Each of these 'disorders' has been well aired in previous commissions. 'This genre', writes Hadley Freeman, 'has nothing to do with journalists opening a window into what life is like for women today. It does women no favours at all. It is entirely about perpetuating an editor's misogynistic image of what women are like (self-hating, self-obsessed)...I have no doubt that the women who write these articles truly feel the emotions they describe. But these women need help; they do not need to be made to feel that their professional USP is to play up their misery' (*The Guardian* 1 July 2009).

Freeman worries that the faux humiliation of the personal columnist, which becomes the fem-humiliation in some confessional writing, 'sets feminism back by about 50 years, because not only does it perpetuate offensive stereotypes about women as needy, helpless, childlike narcissists, it suggests that the most interesting thing a woman can offer up to others is her own battered, starved, bloated, enhanced or reduced body. And that seems a lot sadder to me than any shocking revelation I ever read in a single piece of confessional journalism'. Jill Parkin concurs, 'Writing like this robs you of your professionalism and dignity, turning you into the story. If you keep feeding this monster, eventually it eats you. There is nothing left for you to write about; you have exposed yourself in the most degrading way, opening your wounds; and the commissioning editors will simply turn to fresher tortured flesh' (*The Guardian* 27 April 2009).

Ethics

The consequences of confessional journalism extend further than stereotyping. Confessional journalism also has a problem with the representation of the private lives of others. Of course this is not a new issue for autobiographical writing nor is it exclusive to journalism. The consequences can be pretty catastrophic, even for the novelist, as Lionel Shriver revealed in a confessional piece about how 'I sold my family for a novel' (*The Guardian* 17 October 2009). A recent discussion on Radio 4's Start the week (12 March 2012) was devoted to accounts of personal conflicts which had been created by writing about your own family and friends. All the writers admitted to feelings of being in control over how events got represented. Most expressed some regret at causing distress. But one novelist, A.S. Byatt, confessed that controlling the version of events was sometimes 'thrilling'. Yet this remains an explosive issue for confessional journalism since its stock in trade is intimate revelations and taboo subjects. It's a version of the same issue which has put tabloid journalism under such scrutiny around phone hacking – the degree of consent given to having your personal life and details in print.

The Myerson 'scandal' described in the introduction to this book, which broke around the too-explicit account of her teenage son in 'The Lost Child', followed by revelations that she was also the anonymous, but fairly easily identified, author of the hugely revealing column, 'Living with Teenagers', provoked a degree of soul-searching among many journalists too. *Daily Mail* journalist, Tom Utley, author of a column about family life, 'A Father Writes', ruefully admitted it was all too easy to get it wrong. 'All I can say is that you have to stare at a blank computer screen, with the sub-editors glaring at the clock and the prospect of £350 dangling before you, to understand the family columnist's irresistible temptation to overstep the mark' (cited in Matthew Bell *The Independent* 15 March 2009). The predominant feeling among fellow columnists however was, as Matthew Bell said, that Myerson had crossed a 'previously carefully observed line' (ibid.). Toby Young, author of *How to Lose Friends and Alienate People*, admitted he writes about his children adding 'They're all under six, but when they get older I will have to establish a ground rule to run anything past them first' (ibid.). Tanya Gold quoted earlier as both a prime example of a confessional writer and a passionate supporter of confessional journalism, also had qualms about Myerson's use of her children for material. 'It's is a golden rule that you can only write about yourself…. If you are writing for money, for self-acceptance, or publicity, you only have the right to explore your own life and nobody else's. I happen to like writing about myself so I do, but Julie Myerson is lying to herself if she thinks she is helping her son by writing. You should consult a psychotherapist before consulting your publisher' (ibid.).

The ferocious response to the revelation that Myerson was also author of the heretofore anonymous column led the *Guardian* to act. Myerson's editor, Becky Gardiner concluded 'What we now know – but did not know then – was that the Myerson family was in the grip of a family crisis. Had I known that, I like to think that I would have put aside my editor's appetite for a great column, and advised Julie not to publish, directing her instead to people who might have been able to help them and their son' (*The Guardian* 10 March 2009). 'The Living with Teenagers' column was withdrawn from the website 'to protect the children's privacy' although many pointed out, the damage was already done. Siobhan Butterworth, readers' editor, suggested editors should no longer 'view the decision to publish private information as purely a matter of parental choice'. The newspaper followed her advice updating their editorial code to cover journalists writing about their children. 'The new provisions contain the advice that where children are old enough, their consent to publication should be sought, and suggest editors consider whether children's identities should be obscured online to protect them from embarrassment or harm as they grow older. Anonymous articles that include significant intrusions into children's private lives without their knowledge or consent need a strong public interest justification' (*The Guardian* 6 July 2009).

These guidelines however only scratch the surface. What of my own mother, with dementia? What is the status of her consent? How old is old enough? The advice for anonymity is also vague. Only a few weeks later, the *Guardian* itself published an article on teenagers who hit their parents. Although the teenagers' names had been changed, the author Christine Lewis used her own name (*The Guardian* 27 June 2009). How difficult would it be to identify those children? Neither the now defunct Press Complaints Commission nor any other newspaper introduced similar guidelines, and while the issue of children is clearly most pressing, there are growing numbers of other 'real-life' conflicts arising from confessional journalism. It's disingenuous for Tanya Gold to defend Liz Jones, for example, while saying that Julie Myerson had crossed a line by writing about her children when numerous people have objected to their often vicious – and recognisable – portrayals in Jones' column.

Fully informed consent is almost impossible to obtain for children who should not really be put in a position to give it and of course they require stricter levels of protection. But the truth is, many of those who write autobiographical, and increasingly confessional, writing talk about the private lives of other individuals from whom they do not have true permission. Liz Jones's husband was able to retaliate against public humiliation with his own column. But there are many other individuals in her columns – relatives, friends and neighbours – some named and some able to identify themselves, or be identified by others, who have been described in Jones' columns as ungrateful, only interested in their own children, failing to reciprocate expensive gifts, hostile, unwelcoming, murderous even as she suggests in 'Shotgun bullies are driving me out of rural haven' (*The Daily Mail* 7 September 2009). Jones has proved herself particularly skilled at staying in control when anyone protests at their treatment as column fodder. She uses her column to answer back usually berating them for persecuting her and for not realising her obligation to tell the truth. 'I have earned my money', she says reflecting on her loneliness, 'oh my God I have earned it, decades spent in the office until 2 am, revealing my soul, losing my dignity and every friend I ever had' (*The Daily Mail* 19 August 2012).

Rachel Royce, ex-wife of broadcaster and columnist Rod Liddle, also wrote graphically about her divorce. One commentator described the ensuing spectacle where each partner revealed intimate and shaming details about the other as 'an unedifying public spectacle of bilious accusations and emotional pornography' (*The Observer* 11 July 2004). Lauren Booth, Cherie Blair's half-sister, was involved in a similar tussle over invading the privacy of her own family. In the *Daily Mail*, Booth related how marital difficulties culminated with her announcing on Facebook that she was now single. Her husband, upset, stormed out and was knocked off his motor bike sustaining life-threatening injuries (*The Daily Mail* 4 May 2009). This article, full of intimate details, was followed by another detailing her husband's injuries and slow recovery. At this point his mother retaliated, comparing Lauren Booth unfavourably with another woman who had also written about a husband's accident. 'His wife ... went to great lengths to preserve her husband's dignity. I only wish my daughter-in-law would respectfully do the same for my son while he is still in such a vulnerable state, and that she will cease writing such articles about him' (*The Daily Mail* 11 July 2009).

When Rachel Cusk's highly detailed and intimate account of her divorce was widely serialised, it provoked not just a huge twitter and online storm but also widespread debate among journalists about what rights confessional journalists have to expose the lives of others: 'While "the personal may be political"', says Yvonne Roberts, 'attach a tannoy, and all manner of furies are unleashed and rights abrogated, not least of the children, ex-husbands, siblings and friends, the jackdaw journalist's, often involuntary, supporting cast. These people have no say over the telling of what is their story too. Their privacy is invaded, their most painful moments are exposed to the world' (*The Guardian* 25 February 2012). 'If writers are going to write about their personal lives, they have two conflicting responsibilities', said Tim Lott, 'they have to be scrupulously honest, but they do have to protect the parties involved' (*The Guardian* 25 February 2012).

Lott went on to point out how difficult it is for the confessional journalist writing about their 'children, or partner or ex-partner'; at this 'level of intimacy the lines of separation between yourself and the others you are including in the narrative are blurred'. 'Indeed it is', concurred Christa d'Souza in dialogue with him, saying on the whole she comes down on the side of truth, whatever the consequences. 'The truth is paramount and I can be most truthful about myself. I care less about my partner because he's inured to it. He knows I write about myself. My kids I worry about more, with parents of other kids reading it and making snide comments.' 'You have to try to get approval from the people you're writing about', says Lott arguing for a 'rough and ready ethics'. 'It's wrong to stomp on people because you have the power to do it. I've got it wrong before. It's hard when you have put yourself out there, and you've possibly risked things with friends or relationship. I've suffered a lot of unhappiness as a result of the stuff I've written, but I go on writing it because that's what I do, and I'm proud of it as pieces of writing, but it can be a high stakes game.'

Ethical guidelines for this writing are slow in coming probably for the reasons Lott suggests, that the 'right' to represent your own family is not easy to define. In the circumstances, various conventions have been appearing to circumvent the outright disasters attached to playing 'this high stakes game'. Most noticeable is the way authors continue to write about their children and partners but avoid naming them and create 'successive' roles for the people they write about. Tim Dowling writes about son 1, son 2, etc. who always outsmart him and a wife who is always one step ahead. They are caricatures and largely flattering ones but it would not be hard for their peers to identify them. Zoe Williams writes about 'Baby T', and Lucy Mangan's husband is known throughout as 'Tory Boy'. The end result is a strange merger of the depersonalised with the highly self-revelatory. Some writers, like Tim Dowling, incorporate questions of how much the people written about actually know about the column while Liz Jones, as mentioned earlier, is the master of self-referentiality, constantly exposing, analysing and usually dismissing peoples' objections to how they appear in the columns. In a particularly dizzying week (16 November 2012), both Dowling and Jones wrote columns about appearing together on a panel about the pitfalls of writing about your private life, Jones dismissing Dowling for saying his life is basically alright when the whole point of this confessional writing is to explore misery, while Dowling merely constructs Jones as another one who outsmarts him. In other words, both stick closely to their generic requirement.

Faux personas are relatively harmless if recognised as generic conventions but the faux persona can slide into falsehoods and again Liz Jones appears to be at the forefront. Jones always justifies her inclusion of details which other journalists would balk at as a journalist's obligation to be honest. Nevertheless some have suggested she, too, is capable of evasion and invention. For most of her columns on her rural life, she complains of extreme isolation, but another journalist interviewing her noticed her sister appeared to be living with her (Rachel Cooke *The Observer* 2 August 2009). Shortly after this interview, Jones mentioned for the first time that her sister was staying. For the first few years, her life at the farm was described as deeply isolated, where she never changed out of wellington boots and let her appearance go as she hauled bales of hay around the yard. Yet simultaneously other articles by Jones would appear elsewhere in the newspaper showing her to be travelling to fashion shows, experimenting with beauty treatments and reporting from distant locations. When her house sold online commentary was full of disbelief that her farmhouse was so luxuriously appointed bearing no relation to the freezing hovel she so often described. Her account of her relationship with a rock star with whom she has never been spotted or photographed has been accused of being invented.

Conclusion

Throughout this book, I have emphasised the role of the personal voice to elicit and maintain engagement. Columns where writers share difficult material and open themselves up for scrutiny are particularly powerful at doing this, whether the responses are positive or negative. It is easy to see why editors are drawn to this material. Samantha Brick's article provoked nearly 5000 online comments. Liz Jones' account of finally leaving the country had attracted over 1000 on the first day, the largest ever response. This level of attention is what editors dream of and it's easy to see how it would feed the appetite for this kind of writing.

This is not to disparage confessional writing. As I have made clear, this kind of writing has a history and an important one at that. It is writing which, when it is good, is unbeatable. It deals with the emotions which make us who we are, and the issues that matter – childbirth, relationships, illness, grief. This writing humanises the news, illuminates why events matter and what impact they have on lives. An article in the *Observer* on 'The Nightmares never go away. How Hillsborough changed our lives' (19 March 2009) makes us understand just how devastating the event, and its misrepresentation in the press, was and why the families still want emotional closure. It is also democratising, exposing how the ordinary people's stories are as important as those of the powerful.

It is also a form of journalistic writing that is relatively new, and has become widespread very quickly as newspapers have struggled to find a new role in the era of online news. So the conventions are just developing, as the example of the Myerson scandal demonstrates. A new balance is still to be found between the creation of a fictional persona and the need, at some level at least, to be truthful. The case of Liz Jones demonstrates that both columnists and their readers currently have difficulty in treading this line. And until this balance develops further, the appetite for extreme revelations, for stories which provoke fury as much as quiet empathy, will continue to favour writers with pronounced exhibitionist tendencies because writing which encourages voyeurism is extremely attractive to exhibitionists. Voyeurism is the pleasure of witnessing, while exhibitionism is the pleasure of getting attention by stripping off in public, if not physically at least emotionally. Both voyeurism and exhibitionism are in mild ways part of our whole culture – cinema and television are both built around them – but in extreme forms, they are pathologies. It's hard not to suspect this is the case in some of the more visible and prolific confessional writers, who, in removing layer after layer of skin, reveal not the universals of human responses but merely an exhibitionist personality. Perhaps again it is Liz Jones who articulates and exemplifies this: 'Artists – and I'm sorry but I do consider myself an artist – have to wrench the dirtiest, most disgusting part of their inner soul, and show it to the world, so others can make of it what they will'.

6 Blogging and the Intimate Universality of Cyberspace

'Blogging is not about professional journalism', said Arianna Huffington, justifying the non-payment of contributors as she launched the Quebec Huffington Post site (cited in *The Globe* and *Mail* 8 February 2012). 'Blogging is about self-expression, when you want, if you want', she continued. 'You can write about anything you want for as long as you want, a hundred words or thousands of words.... The important thing is self-expression. Self-expression is the new entertainment and a major source of fulfillment, and we need to understand that... (It's) going to become the new reality.' The success of the web and the threat it poses to old forms of journalism, in becoming the preferred form of information, is fundamentally connected with this personal and personality-led form of communication. It is estimated there are now over a million bloggers. It is personal, opinionated and intimate communication which now draws the readers and increasingly, the money.

Arianna Huffington set up the Huffington Post from scratch in 2005, selling it only a few years later in 2011 for 315 million dollars to the *New York Times*. This fortune has been based on her understanding of the new reality where personal expression and strong opinion draw readers more easily than traditional forms of journalism, where publishers can rely on virtually free input and, compared with traditional media, extraordinarily low costs. When she set up the Huffington Post, many mocked her, recalling how, in the 1970s, her anti-feminist views and relationship with right-wing commentator Bernard Levin made her seem out of synch with the times. After that she'd drifted even further from the mainstream, marrying a rich Republican, Michael Huffington, and absorbing herself in American right-wing politics. In a key speech, 'Newspapers in the Age of Blogs' given in 2006, *Guardian* editor, Alan Rusbridger, examined the rise of Internet journalism and its effect on traditional journalism. He described how Huffington's blog site idea was originally greeted with tolerant amusement: 'Her husband, didn't make

it as President and so she left him and decided that she was a demo-
crat after all and moved to New York and said "I've heard all about this
blogging. I'm going to start a blogging site." And my how they laughed.
Silly little Arianna; what a fluff head; this is just another vanity vehicle
for Arianna. This will be dead in six months. She launched it last May
and they're not laughing now' (Rusbridger 2006, p. 10).

Perhaps Huffington was lucky, but she was certainly quick to recognise
what she had stumbled on. A site made up primarily of blogs not only
gave the contributors freedom to say what they wanted in the way they
wanted, but it also allowed contributors and readers to set the agenda,
reflecting the direction already taken by the Internet towards interactiv-
ity between readers and contributors. Blogging not only allows anyone
the freedom to speak their mind but also gives a sense to both writer
and reader that this is a one-to-one exchange. The sense that writers can
know who they are addressing while readers can feel they have input
and are being addressed personally was, Huffington correctly realised,
satisfying to both.

It was a smart move financially as well. This was a site which didn't
have the expensive task of gathering news directly but mainly com-
mented on that news. And it wasn't just a matter of not paying
expensive journalists; the bloggers didn't have to be paid either. A site
that provides a platform for writers, ensuring that their views would
be communicated and a feeling that they were reaching individuals
directly, turned out to be compensation enough for many; they could
write at the length they chose, on the subject they chose and have their
views posted almost instantaneously. As regards fees, contributors would
be compensated by attracting the attention of others who mattered to
them (politicians and the public). The status given by being in the centre
of the debate, seen by potentially far greater numbers than readers of
newspapers, would generate its own returns in terms of public profile
and brand.

Opinion led, and subjective in tone and style, The Huffington Post is
still ostensibly a news site albeit news scraped from other sources. But
the key to its success, which is considerable as it exercises influence on
other news outlets, remains the centrality it has given to personal views
in the form of blogs. Everything on the site is framed by blogs. Some
are one-off personal opinion columns, some are ongoing political commentary and some, in lifestyle sections, are more intimate narratives,
based on first-person experience. What Huffington harnessed here was
the natural discourse of the web which is also the natural inheritor of
the trends already discussed in this book.

Blogging

Blogging is not only personal in that the opinion and voice of the individual shapes the content, but it also often foregrounds intimate personal material. The vast majority of posts are personal in the broadest sense of the word. Even those blogs and posts which are information or specialist subject-based, like 'techie' sites, usually foreground the personal identity of the writer. If in the past it was journalistic authority, located in the identity of the publication, which guaranteed reasons for listening or reading, now it's the personality. The voice of wisdom, issuing impersonally from the authoritative newspaper, has given way to the voice of the intimate individual speaking to you directly. In a telling comment, social media and web tips website, Mashable, praises the techie site 'iamdan.com' saying: 'It's appropriate that the bio page of iamdan.com begins, "hi. i am dan." It kind of makes you want to say "hi" back.... It's a human being saying "I like this"' (http://mashable.com/2010/09/15/creative-blogger-bio-pages/). This is no longer an impersonal organisation, a newspaper or a publisher, standing between the reader and writer, selecting and sometimes filtering. Like Facebook and Twitter, all social networking share this characteristic of appearing to be the voice of one individual directly addressing another. If the characteristic mode of the press as fourth estate was the voice of one to many, this is the fifth estate, the individual-to-individual mode of address, making the reader feel directly addressed. Or as top blogger and installation artist ZeFrank (Zefrank.com) so cunningly welcomes website visitors, 'many have come but I like you best'.

Recognising the shift towards an expectation of a more personalised presence in journalism, many of the main media organisations, while delivering 'objective news' and reportage in the conventional way, now ask their journalists to write blogs or tweet in a more subjective personal way. Nick Robinson, the BBC's senior political reporter, or Nick as he is known in the intimate language of the blogosphere, was one of the first to adopt blogging in 2001 and he is still found commenting daily in a much more personal, relaxed and chatty manner than is normal in broadcasts, trying to convey that sense to the reader that it's a real person talking directly to them as an individual. All journalism students are now encouraged to keep their own blogs and to find not just their own distinctive subject but also a persona or identity to make themselves stand out from the crowd.

But a professional journalist is just one voice among many on the Internet. Anyone can post and large numbers do. It's estimated there are well over a million active bloggers. If you can catch a reader's attention, you can have it. Bloggers with no journalistic background have garnered huge followings. Blogs 'challenge conventional notions of who is a journalist and what journalism is' (Regan 2003). This is the reason why commentators talk about democratisation. This democratisation of the Internet of which blogging is just one element – alongside citizen journalism, entrepreneurial start-ups, purveying news and info and hyperlocal sites – is the subject of much debate among professionals and academics (Allan 2006; Jarvis 2011; Rusbridger 2006). For many, this democratic space of self-expression is to be celebrated like Leadbeater (2009), who argues that digital media and social networking challenge the old hierarchies of an elitist media by allowing anyone to communicate with anyone in any context. Other likeminded commentators (Tunney 2009) point to the use of social media, blogging and twitter, in wars or during political uprisings where the Internet has provided a forum for voices which might never have been heard in the past. The Iraqi blogger 'Salam Pax' (Salam Abdulmunem) wrote a series of blogs during and after the second Iraq invasion describing, in ways no Western journalism could, the daily experiences of Iraqis as the war waged around them.

Rusbridger (2006, p. 6) describes this as a shift from a time where journalists thought 'our job is to tell you what's what' to a time where the established media no longer controls the conversation. It's no longer in the exclusive power of the established media to direct the conversation by determining who gets to speak, and about what. The new conversations are going on outside, and it doesn't really matter what the established media thinks about this. According to Rusbridger this is a fait accompli, representing a definitive shift of power to readers who can now have conversations with each other, select what they are interested in, start their own blogs or websites where they can focus on what interests them, in short create their own communities. Rusbridger agrees with Huffington: writers and readers coming to these sites have a different motivation. Occasionally, he says, referring to the *Guardian* blog site, Comment is Free, 'when we commission a piece, we pay a modest sum but most people are just coming into this space because this is a wonderful platform for argument and engagement and so forth'(ibid., p. 10). Like Huffington, Rusbridger accepted from an early stage this is the new reality of the Internet and that this new reality had dealt a fundamental blow to one of the tenets on which traditional notions of journalism are built, namely the idea of journalism as the voice of authority from on high. Democratisation of opinion means anyone can say anything, nobody can determine in advance what should and should not be discussed and people can talk directly to each other without mediation.

Not everyone is as positive, and certainly not about the aspects of blogging which are my focus, that is the highly personal discourse of blogs including the 'personal life-story blogs'. For alongside all the information-based websites and new 'alternative' news websites and the political or social issue blogs, there are many hundreds of thousands of bloggers for whom personality is not just an element providing transparency about who is speaking, but an end in itself. These are bloggers who have simply decided to share their daily lives with strangers. Any click almost anywhere on the Internet on any subject will take you right into the middle of these personal stories. It might be a day-to-day account of a sex worker, or the musings of a woman about what she will cook for her husband tonight, or the latest from a family attempting to lead the good life in the countryside. But whatever the ostensible subject, the ups and downs, hopes and disappointment, all the intimate thoughts and especially feelings will be there for anyone to read. Personal blogging is the natural inheritor of the developments examined in previous chapters, and takes it to the next level. Intimate and confessional journalism, as we have seen, has made personal experiences and personality ever more present in conventional journalism. But on the Internet it has become the dominant form. While there are hundreds of thousands of blogs on every subject under the sun, the key elements for the vast majority, even those on serious social and political subjects, are the personal voice, the personal viewpoint and the personality of the writer.

Confessional blogging

Among the top blogs at the time of writing are numerous confessional intimate blogs. There are hundreds of 'Mommy blogs' (US) and 'Mummy blogs' (UK) about children and family life. There are blogs about ongoing situations like illness or divorce as in Stephanie Klein's 'Greek tragedy', an uninhibited account of a painful divorce (stephanieklein.com). There are food blogs like 'eatlikeagirl.com', mixing a personal diary with cooking tips. There are sex diaries like 'girlwithaonetrackmind.com', which the author insists is all based on her 'real life' and 'and all true'. There are fashion blogs like 'thestylerookie.com' written by teenagers like Tavi Gevison's. There's Johnny B's 'privatesecretdiary.com' which as the *Guardian* noted is 'neither private nor terribly secret', a mundane blog about a family living in the country, or belgianwaffling.com, a similarly low-key blog about an English woman bringing up her children in Belgium. The world's most read blog comes into this category. In 2007, Chinese actress-turned-director Xu Jinglei became the world's most widely read blogger logging 100 million page views with blog.sina.com.cn/xujinglei. In 2011, it passed the one billion followers. Xu Jinglei writes not only about how she's feeling, her travels and her social life but also about many details of her daily life typically entering: 'finally the first kitten's been born!!! Just waiting for the second, in the middle of the third one now!!!!!!!! It's midnight, she gave birth to another one!!!!!!' Every post produces literally hundreds of comments from readers, 'affirming their love, offering advice, insisting she take care' (*The Observer* 9 March 2008).

These sorts of blogs make up a significant, perhaps the most significant, type of blogging. But they hardly lend themselves to grandiose political claims of helping widen democracy, and whereas many critics rally to defend the political bloggers, most unite in dismissing this kind of personal blogging. Given the snobbery I have described earlier among some writers who pour scorn on the subjective, personal and intimate writing as opposed to the serious, 'objective', detached writing of 'proper' journalism, this is hardly surprising. The Internet is seen by them as the ultimate manifestation of these tendencies: dangerously unrestrained, subjective, a babel of unmediated, personalised, opinionated commentary. It is the confessional medium par excellence. Moreover, it is seen as not just personalised and opinionated but completely personal, looking no further than the world beyond the home's immediate four walls. Keen (2007) calls the Internet 'the cult of the amateur' and claims 'It's all about digital narcissism, shameless self-promotion. I find it offensive.'

If some of the writers like Liz Jones and Rachel Cusk, discussed in the previous chapter, seem solipsistic, self-engrossed and exhibitionistic, some personal blogs on the Internet make Cusk's and Jones' writing seem not just crafted but positively restrained. Diane's Under An Olive Tree is a randomly chosen, but typical, example of these solipsistic blogs. Unlike others blogs mentioned so far, this hasn't commanded any significant following, indeed rarely more than 17 followers, which is hardly surprising given the unmediated, and narratively chaotic, stream of detail. The experience is like stepping into a family round robin – un-self-conscious and intimate details about people whose names we don't recognise and whose lives don't stand up to being described in huge detail. In one passage the writer, after apologising for 'the four month blogging hiatus', gallops into an incomprehensible and exhaustive account of the family's recent miseries. 'The cardiologist said that with Pio's symptoms (they were predictable, repeatable, etc.) he needed to go straight in for the cardiac cath. OK, then we started thinking that Pio might need a stent because he was often out of breath with little exertion – and it no longer seemed obvious that it was his asthma acting up. Long story short – the catheterization showed four blockages – including one in the main descending artery (the "widow maker" – 60% blocked) and he was scheduled for a bypass operation the following day, November 18.' And so it goes on.

Not all personal blogs are as poorly expressed and relentlessly un-self-aware, while simultaneous self-obsessed as this, nevertheless Under An Olive Tree embodies many key blogging characteristics: highly personal, unrestrained confessions talking to the blog as if everything is of interest, pouring her heart out and foregrounding her feelings. Yet it is clearly short-sighted to dismiss all personalised blogging as 'digital narcissism'. This first-person based, intimate voice is the Internet's characteristic mode of communication, and to resist it is a bit like King Canute trying to hold back the tide. No amount of head shaking by media theorists will put this genie back in the bottle, not least because people have realised that building websites around personal blogs is one of ways in which money can be made from the web. To dismiss this form of writing is short-sighted because personal blogging is the natural successor to the cultural impulses explored elsewhere in this book, that is the growing urge to display and witness intimate life events as well as foregrounding the personality who is speaking. The Internet has provided the place where those impulses are centre stage, accessible to all, either as people who post or follow, and a failure to engage with these forms means ignoring this major cultural form. More seriously, to ignore these outputs leaves a glaring gap in our critical understanding. Blogs like any other form of literature and journalism rely on literary devices and have their own aesthetic conventions; there are good and bad examples and, like the literature and journalism in this area, there are many ethical dilemmas about the airing of personal issues.

Confessional blogging: Conventions and dilemmas

Justin Hall is often credited with being the first blogger, a student who started posting to fellow 'techies' in an academic context. He is also an extreme example of the confessional blogger, highlighting the symbiotic link between the Internet and this form of writing. Was it the confessions which drew the readers to the site or was it that Hall, like several of the early bloggers, hit on the key purpose right from the beginning? Whichever it was, Hall's blogs embody the story of Internet blogging – how it emerged, how it is used, its literary conventions and its ethical dilemmas.

Justin Hall started his blog, 'Justin's links' (links.net), in 1994 when aged 19 and a student at Swarthmore, at a time 'when the www was a flashy new precinct on the obscure, mostly academic computer network known as the intranet, which was then inhabited mostly by grad students, scientists and a handful of precocious teens' (Scott Rosenberg *The Guardian* 13 March 2011). 'My name is Justin Allyn Hall', he announced, 'I was bread [*sic*] and spread in Chicago (the city proper dammit!). During the academic year, I attend Swarthmore College in Pennsylvania. I recently took a semester off to work as an Editorial Assistant at HotWired – a genuine card-carrying member of their digital revolution. I'm a Sagittarius/Pisces rising (check out my chart), born on the same day as Beethoven, in the year of Watergate. This web stuff really inspires me because I can publish me, or anyone else, without having to satisfy any external requirements. No publication or distribution costs!' A prescient comment if ever there was one.

Hall was typical of early users – a bit techie, a bit isolated. In the early Internet, he saw not just a way of pursuing his fascination with the new technology but also an opportunity to share his life. Hall began posting onto his site at Links.net. 'Building a hypertext edifice of autobiography, a dense thicket of verbal self-exposure leavened with photos and art' (Rosenberg ibid.). Along with 'cool' stuff he had found on the Internet, he posted pictures of aunts and uncles, cross referencing with links to back history and explanations of their lives. In January 1996, he was dared by friends to start daily postings and hundreds of readers came to the site. The site had occasional nude photos and links to other interesting sites. But most of the followers came for 'the spectacle of a reckless young man pushing at the boundaries of the new medium in every direction' (Rosenberg ibid.).

According to Scott Rosenberg, a blogger and historian of blogging himself (Rosenberg 2009), Hall's 'confessional ethos was from the start absolute'. Along with accounts of what he eats for dinner he exposed his sexual fantasies and encounters, details of medical procedures and introduced us to his relatives, from which it was a small step to the details of his father's suicide. The self-lacerating, self-exposing details are reminiscent of the most extreme confessional journalists mentioned earlier, especially the readiness to reveal details which most of us might consider far too intimate to reveal. An example was 'a graphic report of a genital infection Hall contracted on a trip to Japan – even his most thick skinned followers might have blanched' (Rosenberg 2011). In the following years, Hall's following increased rapidly attracted presumably by his relentless self-exposure. Hall says 'What's got me pumped is my autobio, tellin' stories about my life'. Rosenberg (ibid.) has called him 'a provocative exhibitionist'. But Hall is also a good writer, who tells a good story, with drama, suspense and humour as well as playing with Internet forms, making good use of links and photos and sometimes even poems.

It was inevitable that someone so thoroughgoingly exhibitionistic ran into the ethical dilemmas connected with revealing so much of his life. Hall's was the first blog to vividly foreground how involving others in your autobiographical revelations had exactly the same implications on the Internet as in publishing or conventional journalism. All these outlets raise the issue of the consent of people who are included in the writer's version of events. After several postings about a developing relationship, Hall suddenly removed them all and replaced them with a video made in film noir confessional style about meeting a woman who was not happy about being written about – an interesting, possibly exemplary decision, about the rights of others over their own story. Hall is astute about the consequences of his actions and could give lessons to other confessional writers and bloggers about them: 'I published my life on the f'ing internet and it doesn't make people want to be with me it makes people not trust me' (*The Guardian* 13 March 2011). In one sentence, Hall understands what Liz Jones constantly fails to see – why people object to her inclusion of them in her personal narrative. Hall understands that his exhibitionism makes him dangerous.

Rosenberg (*The Guardian* 13 March 2011) describes Hall's dilemmas about how much to invade other's privacy as symptoms of blogging's teething problems, brought about by having to learn where to draw a line between what is public and what is private. These problems, he suggests, previously only affected royalty and celebrities whose lives attracted so much interest. Now, he says, with the Internet everyone is in danger of blurring the boundaries between public and private. 'Today thanks to blogs, Facebook, and all the other web-borne opportunities for self-publishing, this burden now falls on all of us' (ibid.). As we've seen in previous chapters, this problem is endemic in all autobiographical writing and especially confessional journalism. More to the point, as the Leveson Committee has highlighted, tabloid journalism has for many decades now been interested in the lives of ordinary people, using them for their moral tales. All these areas are troubled by the same issue of where to draw the line between public and private.

Justin Hall was alert to this minefield from a fairly early stage in his blogging career, but it hasn't stopped him. More recently, he has separated from his wife and on a 2012 post revealed intimate details. 'I haven't really been on a date in a while. I've been busy! And I have felt too raw – on the first flight to Chicago the flight attendant was very helpful, filling my water bottle and it felt so nice to have a pretty woman be nice to me I wanted to cry. Heh – a little too much of a hole in my heart to undertake casual coupling. I have actually felt shy about approaching appealing candidates which is not usually my problem. Though horniness, what you might call life force, won't let me rest long' (links.net). He has also been exploring his grief at the death of his stepfather sharing all the details of his emotional life. 'I thought I would numb my grief with whiskey and weed. Shortly afterwards I found myself on my knees sobbing. It's been months since I have felt that kind of physical grief!' (ibid.).

Hall's motivation is probably more exhibitionistic than commercial and he defends his activities in terms strikingly relevant to this book. His blogging, he says, is not only therapeutic for himself but also possibly for his readers. 'At my site, I encourage personal publishing, dispense advice, and give guided tours of the web. Cuz I've been publishing and receiving feedback since January 1994, I got oodles of love to give back to the net. Sharing stories gives guidance. Hearin' my grampa reflect on death sure made me appreciate life. Young folks going to get a little different spin on sexually transmitted diseases when they hear from another 20-year-old who caught an STD. I was arrested, felonied and strip searched for taking notes on a protest. Read about it, it should piss you off too. I'll talk to anyone who'll listen. Joy and pain is pretty universal; maybe you'll find catharsis or a sense of yourself within. Other folks are sharing their life too, some following my example' (links.net). But it is also a way of rendering information transparent. Instead of communications issuing from unknown sources, his communications show exactly where he is coming from. 'As best I see it, this is the least alienating incarnation of this medium. No distance, no bullshit objectivity; I'm telling stories about my life; you can either take it or leave it. I'm not going to tell you have to read it to be hip, I'm not saying I'm the authority on anything but what I been through. Real stories, or personally inflected stories, ring true because I don't deny myself a place in them. You know where I stand, so you know where you stand. And perhaps your father also died when you were young. Or you had trouble relating to a beautiful person with whom you were in love. Or you got the best job you could possibly imagine, and didn't want to work there anymore' (ibid.).

This is a key statement about the personalised utterances of the Internet, but it also reveals a central paradox. The Internet allows the blogger to thoroughly reveal himself or herself, but one reason bloggers often give for being able to speak so personally is that the Internet feels impersonal when they are writing. They may talk as if they are addressing an individual, but they are not speaking directly to that individual. Conversation with another individual would introduce inhibitions, just as imagining an editor's reaction in a newspaper might inhibit the personal columnist. Online, by contrast, there appears to be a disinhibition effect: 'that feeling so many of us have that we can get away with saying things online that we'd never dream of saying in person. Maybe we believe this because we think we're anonymous. Maybe we think that the web is somehow unreal or disconnected from the rest of our lives. Or maybe... we think that people who might resent what we're saying will never see it' (Rosenberg *The Guardian* 13 March 2011).

Another of the early successful bloggers, and someone who has made a huge commercial success out of blogging is Heather Armstrong, and her experiences give interesting insight into some of the dilemmas created by the Internet's tendency to disinhibit the speaker. When Heather started writing her blog (dooce.com) in February 2001, she was Heather Hamilton, 25 years old, employed by a start-up company exploring the potential of this new medium which was still, at that point, mainly an academic resource. She was unmarried and her first post, a polemic against religion, was just after 9/11. She followed it up with posts on her reasons for her views: she had been brought up as Mormon and wrote about struggling to 'shed the harm' of a Mormon upbringing. Her style was wry, witty and indiscreet, often giving real people who featured in the columns joke names. This landed her in trouble when she started posting comments online about her work colleagues. At that point, Armstrong believed her posts would not be seen by her bosses; she referred to her boss as the Vice President of Spin. Needless to say, he was not pleased and she was sacked.

Armstrong's error was pretty understandable. When she started posting, the Internet was still very much a minority tool and she had no particular reason to realise that the people she was writing about would see it. Armstrong's blog was called dooce.com (which grew out of a typo for dude) and the name has become synonymous in America with this particular Internet pitfall. 'Dooced' is now a commonly used term meaning losing your job as a result of online indiscretions about work. Just after she lost her job, Armstrong wrote 'BE YE NOT SO STUPID. Never write on the internet about work unless your boss knows.' Most know this now but many users are only just learning the same lesson with Facebook.

Armstrong was pretty horrified at her own naivety but, in blog terms, this was a good career move. Her blog took off when, as a result of the sacking, she moved back to Salt Lake City shortly after having proposed to her future husband Jon (who was also jobless) appropriately via the comment section of his blog days before she was fired. Back in Salt Lake City, she temporarily moved back into her mother's basement. Feeling depressed, she decided to continue blogging, allowing herself the 'freedom to explore my emotions', although perhaps now a little bit more savvy about the Internet: 'I will never write anything', she said in a telling remark, 'that I wouldn't say to your face with fifty people watching'.

These life setbacks, all recounted in self-exposing detail, attracted readers. But the real increase came when she announced she was pregnant. The birth of her daughter in 2004 coincided with a time of huge growth in the numbers of bloggers and websites. Like Hall, Armstrong's was one of the first blogs which showed readers would click through for updates from a personal life. It was one of earliest successful personal narratives and the first, and still most significant, in the phenomenon known as 'mommy bloggers'. Armstrong's is classic confessional writing, sometimes wry and humorous, sometimes emotionally revealing, but often dealing with difficult issues such as losing her job, regressing to her childhood home, rejecting the values she grew up with. 'It was a life lived as a cautionary tale', says Lisa Belkin, herself a successful blogger (*New York Times* February 2001), 'a daily reality show on the smaller screen. Readers had begun to show they would click through for breaking news, Hollywood gossip and "techie" inside info but now they would come to hear a blogger say what others might have thought or feared or wondered but just kept to themselves'.

Heather Armstrong has no reasons to regret initial mistakes. She remains one of the most successful personal bloggers and these days has a highly sponsored commercially backed website. This site feels very different from her early ruminations on her personal life. It carries ads for IKEA, sometimes with Heather herself plugging products. Now her personal blog draws in hundreds of thousands of readers and delivers them to the advertisers or sponsors. According to Belkin (ibid.) what started as a therapeutic personal diary is now a business and, although still run from her home, she's the president. On the 2011 Forbes List of most influential women in the media, Armstrong was number 26, just one place below Tina Brown. 'Her site brings in an estimated $30–$50,000 a month or more – and that's not even counting the revenue from her two books, healthy speaking fees and the contracts she's signed to promote Verizon and appear on HGTV' (Belkin ibid.). 'Although her exact final income is not known, the company which sells ad space on her site hinted that their most successful bloggers can gross $1 million.' But many followers dislike it. 'Now I just see those posts', grumbles one follower, 'as free advertising (although maybe that's an assumption!) Or filler on days when Heather doesn't have time to put up other content' (dooce.com).

Armstrong's blogging also demonstrates a fundamental truth about privacy today. In these days of exhibitionism and voyeurism, your private life is a commodity and can be commercialised. There are numerous examples now of bloggers getting book contracts, or creating financially viable websites, like British secretary, Catherine Sanderson, who in 2004 in Paris happened upon the concept of blogging and went on to create one of the most successful blogs 'petiteanglaise.com'. She picked up a large number of followers as she told of her life in Paris, the strained relationship with her partner and bringing up a child in Paris. 'And there was plenty of drama to watch', says Belkin (ibid.), 'within a year her relationship had broken up, and she'd met a new man who wooed her online'. 'I set up this blog in July 2004', the bio page of Sanderson's blog tells us, 'A year later, I left my partner, Mr. Frog, the father of my daughter Tadpole, for a man I met in my comments box, documenting everything here' (petiteanglaise.com). Readers were gripped by her unflinching dedication to telling the whole story, no matter how she would be judged. Soon afterwards, however, Sanderson's employers found out about the blog and promptly fired her. But hers is a blogger morality tale. The bad ('In 2006 I got dumped, dooced and outed') can become the good ('but also landed a book deal'). She won her case against her employers for unfair dismissal and scored a lucrative two-book deal with Penguin.

Blogging may take place in a new space – the Internet – and have many distinct and novel aspects. But it has elements that are also decidedly familiar. Lisa Belkin, who writes a mommy blog for the *New York Times*, has described the confessional form which underlies Armstrong's and Sanderson's successes as 'a meeting of 18th century journalising, 19th century magazine serials and the intimate universality of cyberspace' (Belkin *New York Times* February 2011). Perhaps she should have said seventeenth century because there are striking similarities between some of these blogs and one of the most famous diaries in the English Language, the *Diary of Samuel Pepys*. Pepys chronicled the events in life in exactly the same way as these contemporary confessionals, including the highly personalised details such as a graphic account of his wife having her ear wax removed after she became deaf. One wonders if she might have felt like one of Hall's supporting cast if she had known this might ever be widely read.

The parallels are so striking between Pepys's diary and contemporary blogging that in 2003 a website was set up to publish Pepys' diary as a blog (Pepysdiary.com). There were regular 'postings' of episodes, eliciting and getting comments from 'followers', albeit of a rather scholarly kind, filling in and debating certain references and it won the 'best specialist blog' in the *Guardian*'s Best of British blogs award in 2003. The urge to confess all on a blank page or screen is not a new one and has an honourable tradition in the pantheon of literature. Pepys' diaries were not published until a century after his death, but the fact he preserved them safely suggests not only did they fulfil the same therapeutic impulse described by all the confessional journalists and bloggers discussed in this book, but that he recorded history and personal life with a sense of recording his life for posterity. Some contemporary bloggers talk of the same dual motivation; getting it of their chest but with an eye to posterity, that their lives should be witnessed.

Nowhere are these motivations and dilemmas writers and readers of personal blogs clearer than in Mommy blogs or Mummy blogs, the genre which Armstrong inhabited. This is one of the biggest areas of blogging and certainly one of the most commercial. There are significant numbers of personal blogs with full sponsorship from nappy brands or formula milk. In the United Kingdom, Mumsnet, a multifunction website with advice, political policy and chat, has 600,000 registered users and regularly hosts debates with leading politicians. Both left and right recognise it as a political force and it draws significant advertising from leading brands. But it is also stitched together down the seams with dozens of personal life blogs, ranging from 'Three children and It' (daily life with three children and their pooch) through 'Frog at Large' (a French woman bringing up children in England) to '21st Century Stay at Home Mum' (self-explanatory).

In the United States, there are numerous 'Mommy blogs' which have now achieved the same level of prominence and success as Heather Armstrong's. Successful, in this context, means not just popular but commercially successful, attracting sponsors and advertising.

Ree Drummond's the pioneerwoman.com is typical. It has a good background premise (urban woman marries a cowboy and raises children on a ranch in the middle of nowhere or as she puts it: 'my long transition from spoiled city girl to domestic country wife'); lots of difficulties (a love affair, a personal struggle of adjustment, the birth of four children, one of whom is ill and another autistic); and a wry self-deprecating take on it all 'Welcome to my frontier! I'm a moderately agoraphobic ranch wife and mother of four...a middle child who grew up on the seventh fairway of a golf course in a corporate town. I was a teen angel. Not.'

The most popular blogs however tend, like confessional journalism, to be about difficulties or better still, tragedies. Dawn Meehan's 'Because I said so.com' started as a humorous chronicle of a mother of six. At the beginning, her About page read: 'Dawn recently moved to Orlando with her six children, where she practices her juggling skills daily. On any given evening, Dawn can be found taking one child to cheerleading practice, dropping off another at church, making dinner, going to the grocery store, paying the bills, kissing a boo-boo, reading a bedtime story, cleaning up muddy footprints, folding laundry, taking a child to the ER, and explaining to her kids why they can't have an indoor Slip 'N Slide or a pet squirrel'. But the column took a dramatic turn resulting in a correspondingly dramatic increase in readers when her husband left her, two of her sons were hospitalised with depression and the family lost their health insurance.

Throughout all this, Meehan adopted the classic faux self-deprecatory blog version of the 'I'm a hopeless sap' columnist, here expressed as 'I'm a rotten Mum', which sometimes sits oddly with the simultaneous self-aggrandisement on the site telling visitors her blog 'was voted the Best Parenting Blog by the Blogger's Choice Awards' and 'nominated for the Best Humour Blog, the Hottest Mommy Blogger, the Best Parenting Blog, and the Best Blog of All Time for the past three years'. As well as nominated for the Funniest Blog by BlogLuxe'. 'Her kids think the blog is just okay', she concludes remembering Russell Frank's dictum that that the personal columnist like the coyote must burn its own arse.

Many other bloggers have been hit by similar tragedies. Katie Allison Granju's blog 'mamapundit.com' started as an account of 'blended family life', that is, two families joined by remarriage. But the relatively upbeat account of the normal complexities associated with this situation turned dark when Kate's 18-year-old son died from a drugs overdose. Katie was herself two weeks away from giving birth when it happened. At the time, she had asked her son to leave home, the plan being to force him back into rehab. In her blog, she writes in painful detail about her regrets at having been so harsh on him and especially at having missed the stream of calls her son made home just before he died. Many posts are about a mother struggling with this loss. She's still writing about the legacy of dealing with his death, but the blog now also includes campaign writing about the need for proper support for teenagers with addiction.

Stephanie Nielson also started her blog (stephanienelson.com) as a rather smug mother of four, writing about nothing out of the ordinary such as her pregnancy and children's sleepovers. But then she and her husband were severely injured in a plane crash. Her husband pulled her, badly burnt, from the wreckage. Her face was severely scarred. Since then, she has continued to blog charting the reconstructive surgery, the family reactions to her injury – including one child running away when she sees her face – the struggle back to health and the birth of a new baby. These blogs attract huge numbers of responses consisting of empathetic comments, offers of advice and personal revelations from the readers about their own tragedies.

Heather Spohr's blog (thespohrsaremultiplying.com), which evolved into a top blog, also as a result of an unexpected tragedy, gives insight into the relationship between these confessions and the 'reader' responses. Spohr started blogging in 2002 but in 2007 launched 'the Spohrs are Multiplying' as a way of updating her family on the progress of her premature baby Maddie. Initially it had a small audience but in April 2009, Maddie unexpectedly died. A friend stepped in to continue the posts informing them, that 'Maddie aged 2 and half had unexpect-edly died'. Readers poured out their sympathy to Heather and a few days later she posted again: 'I am speaking tomorrow at the service for my daughter. The FUNERAL service for MY DAUGHTER. I type the words, and I understand them, but I feel as if I am talking about someone else. I see the emails, the comments, the tweets, the cards, the letters, the donations to the March of Dimes, the articles, the TV stories, and I can't comprehend that it's my daughter that's being talked about. I can't comprehend' (thespohrsaremultiplying.com).

Writing about this decision to speak at the funeral, Heather urges her-self to keep going: 'I will channel all the bravery my Maddie had, all the strength and courage she showed in her too-short life, and I will pay my daughter tribute. As her mommy, I owe her this. If I tell myself enough that I can do it, then maybe I can.' Typically, hundreds responded in highly personalised ways. 'Yes, you can do this', posted 'Monica' for example, 'because there are thousands of people all across the country (perhaps even the world) that love your sweet family and are praying like mad that you'll be able to meet every challenge you face in the days ahead. Oh how I wish I could help shoulder your burden. Oh how every one of us who has been moved by those huge blue eyes wishes we could take a tiny piece of the pain ... god will give you strength tomorrow. And the next day. And the next.'

Because these followers have been recipients of intimate revelations in a very individual way, receiving the communication alone in front of a screen, they feel as if they have a direct connection to the events unfolding. Just as with confessional journalism, it's misery and tragedies which really boost the level of engagement. 'When you hear of the Redneck Mommy', it says on Babble.com when listing its top 'most confessional blogs', 'you might think Deep South. But Tanis Miller is actually from Canada, where she blogs about a life sprinkled with both funny anecdotes and heart-breaking grief. Shortly after the death of one of her children, Miller turned to the internet to let out all of her feelings. And we're glad she did.' The biggest numbers are drawn to the rawest, most taboo, outpourings like VodkaMum about an alcoholic mother. In this respect they share a great deal with both confessional journalism and misery memoirs, which many of the blogs actually become when published in book form, in that they are tales of extreme misery, unkind blows of fate and the struggle to keep going or renew oneself in the face of psychological problems or tragic life events.

Blogs, however, differ from confessional journalism, which is delayed by various editorial processes before it is printed or posted on the news organisation website. Without having to pass through gatekeepers, like editors, lawyers and subs, blogs by contrast can engender a closer relationship with readers, conducted almost in real time. Many social network commentators argue that Twitter is the main real-time information medium (Keen 2007). But 140 characters is not suited to communicate real tragedy and crucially not suited to the exploration of innermost feeling. Blogging, which takes place almost in real time, and at greater length, is much better suited to handle emotional reactions and detailed feelings. 'Oh Heather', posts Tokissthecook on the day the Spohr's tragedy was announced, 'I am beside myself for you. Been offline and the last I saw was ice cream and I'm just so shocked. Sending as many loving thoughts as I can warm together at this point.'

This is clue to one of the key attractions for both writer and reader of these online personal outpourings. It's impersonal but it simulates the intimacy of a one-to-one close friendship: 'It allows a direct link with readers', says Ellie Leveson, a British Mumsnet blogger

(Goodynuffmum.com). This sense of direct link applies to the writer with their readers, to the readers with their chosen bloggers and between readers through 'threads'. It creates a sense of community. It may be a smaller community than a newspaper's readership but for the above reasons it feels more meaningful. Each reader has read attentively and sometimes responded: ' I'd rather an engaged audience of people', continues Leveson, 'who are interested in your subject than the wider audience a newspaper brings who read the first sentence then quickly turn the page'.

English blogger Emma Beddlington is astute about the curious paradoxical nature of personal blogging. Her blog, Belgian waffling, she says 'evolved from a humorous take on living in Belgium into a blog revealing much more difficult and intimate personal details' (Interview with Scott Rosenbaum *The Guardian* 13 March 2011). Started in 2008, Beddlington found she enjoyed 'the sense of community' her blog gave her, with people responding to her humorous take on Belgian eccentricities. 'This encouraged me gradually to write about more personal things, about my mother's death, about living with alopecia, struggling with an eating disorder...I'm reserved to the point of total inarticulacy as a person but on the blog I was able to express things I couldn't possibly say face to face' (ibid.). 'There's a particular candour you get from bloggers that I don't think you get in other kinds of writing. Something about the anonymity – the vastness of the internet gives you the sense that you are whispering your secrets into the void' (ibid.). Rosenbaum calls this 'Digital dis-inhibition'. The posts are not created through interpersonal dialogue but privately, usually alone. The writing doesn't have to pass by anyone – an editor, a publisher, even a friend receiving a letter. It therefore feels more impersonal, less prone to social inhibitions, less embarrassing, less concerned with the other's reactions. It gives a sense that anything can be said. Yet in that anonymous void, readers whisper back, and whisper to each other: a community of anonymous, personalised individuals.

When Samuel Pepys wrote his diary, he had no sense of a community of followers. But he put his dairy into a safe place possibly hoping that one day it would be read, a record of his life, enjoyable to write but, surely for any kind of communicator, better still if read by another as witness to your life. Between Pepys's protection of a personal document and its publication, there were many barriers to cross. It had to be lucky and get preserved. It had to have the protection of others. It had to survive the scrutiny of editors and publishers. Now the Internet abolishes those obstacles. 'Hit the "post" button and any personal writing become published writing' ('Who are your Gatekeepers?' Andrews 2001). But bloggers may have the same impulse which led Pepys to protect his writing, namely the desire to tell your story and have your life witnessed. Reflecting on how her blog evolved from easy updates for family and friends about her premature baby, Spohr explains: 'After that, I wrote so Maddie would have a record of her life. So that someday, when she went through the awkward and unjust parts of growing up, I could say to her, "Honey, you are so tough, this is nothing compared to what you've already faced." ' And now, she continued after Maddie's death, 'Well...WE have a record of her life. If she ever has a sibling, we will be able to say "THIS is your sister." ' Witnessing is not just about watching other people's emotions, it's also claiming some permanence for yourself by witnessing yourself as others see you, in photos in print or in an online blog which is perhaps the strong attraction of blogs for cancer sufferers. It's the same impulse on Facebook and other social media. Keen calls it narcissism, but it could equally be seen as the desire to render oneself immortal through some kind of 'publishing'. Witnessed, published, I have existed.

Personal, intimate, uninhibited, immediate and ongoing, laden with the desire for your life to be witnessed, it shouldn't be surprising that blogs, even more than confessional journalism, are usually seen as raw truth. In addition, because they are not mediated by any news organisation but appear to come directly from the author, they carry all the more heavily the aura of true stories. But this kind of Internet intimacy is no more 'the real truth' than is confessional journalism, nor are blogs any less narrative constructs drawing on literary conventions than confessional journalism.

As with confessional journalism, there is a dominant voice – ranging from wry, hopeless and helpless to troubled and tragic. The voice of the blogger can be any, and all, of these but what they cannot be, if they want a community, is boastful and un-self-aware. This inevitably means the sort of low-level 'lying' involved in these conventions with the same pseudo personality ('oh shoot, the dog's eaten the kids' breakfast again') as the confessional writer as critiqued by Russell Frank (2004). This is not so much lying as writing within genre. The Internet audience is not looking for smug self-satisfaction; they are looking for difficulty, tragedy and want to witness how this tragedy is dealt with. Nor are they looking for someone who talks down to them from their successful life, but for someone who talks across to them as a friend who has the same trials as they have. Indeed preferably worse ones.

There is a distinct preference for certain types of narratives, in particular triumph over tragedy, stories where the narrator emerges from a bad place and either through their own good attitude or luck of a new romance or a new baby or a good move to a new location, triumphs over misery – morality tales in short. There is also a flourishing strand of rags to riches where the blog is itself the route to success, like Catherine Sanderson's la Petite Anglaise.

The anonymity of the Internet adds other complications. The gentle 'fakery' implicit in these conventions can give way to downright lying as in the recent scandal of the Syrian lesbian blogger. The blog, A Gay Girl in Damascus, was launched in February (2012), offering itself as 'what it's like to be a lesbian here'. It achieved a large following, especially as the Syrian uprising spread, offering descriptions of protests and demonstrations as well, inevitably, a strong personal narrative about being forced into hiding because of her lesbian affairs. At one point, her friend claimed she had been kidnapped. But after suspicions grew, and amidst great anger from Syrians who felt it had jeopardised their safety, it was revealed that the blog was a hoax. 'The blogs were written not by a gay girl in Damascus, but a middle-aged American man based in Scotland.' Tom MacMaster defended himself saying, 'While the narrative voice may have been fictional, the facts on this blog are true and not misleading as to the situation on the ground' (*The Guardian* 13 June 2011).

This kind of fakery is by no means unique to blogging. An almost identical scam was pulled years ago when an English vicar, Toby Forward, tricked Virago, the feminist press, into publishing him under the name of Rahila Khan (1987), pretending he was a young Muslim girl. Both these writers entered into the deception as authors of fictions where conventions were relatively easy to learn or put on but there's something about the Internet as a mode of communication which makes this a higher risk. Sherry Turkle (1995) argues that computers and the Internet are redefining human identity, as people explore the boundaries of their personalities, adopt multiple selves and form online relationships that can be more intense than real ones. She talks about the freedoms of the web, and the ability to enter multiple identities playfully. Turkle's work is mainly on chat and games rooms but her ideas have relevance here to the question of anonymity and authentication. The World Wide Web, she says, is redefining our sense of community and where we find our peers. In spite of use for personal ends, in spite of feelings of community, in spite of feelings of being involved in intimate situations, it is potentially the most anonymous of media. Many conventions on the Internet reinforce that anonymity – especially the practices of adopting anonymous identities, fake names and avatars. All of which can be powerfully attractive to certain types of personalities.

Conclusion

As we've seen, one of the key reasons the Internet has been put to such intensely personal use is precisely this anonymity. The online disinhibition effect creates the feeling of being able to get away with saying things we'd never dare to say face-to-face. Yet it is also the case that communicating online feels immediate and personal. The nature of the Internet is not only highly personal, creating the impression of direct unmediated communication, but also simultaneously highly impersonal, since you write as an individual alone with a screen. This creates conditions in which the usual social barriers, whether in relation to workplace etiquette or face-to-face interaction, seem to be lowered. The impulse to bare all on the Internet, to speak so much more openly than you would either at your workplace or in conversation has from the start thrown up new ethical dilemmas, whether the blogs are intimate personal confessions or unguarded personal opinions. Such dilemmas emerged along with the first bloggers and the ground rules of blogging are still being created as each new dilemma is encountered.

Conclusion

This book started with a story and will end with one too. Appropriately, this one will be about myself. I first started writing features regularly in the 1980s, mainly for the *Guardian*, the *New Statesman*, *New Society* and various women's magazines like *Cosmopolitan* and *She*. I also wrote occasional features for the *Daily Telegraph* and arts-based publications. Women's magazines, then, were already carrying 'personal features', covering personal issues, and using an intimate personal address to their readers. For the magazine, *She*, for example, I wrote articles about the conflicting emotions felt by working mothers, of which I was one. But, reviewing that copy from a contemporary perspective, the degree to which personal detail was included seems remarkably restrained. As regards the newspapers, writing like this, covering more intimate issues and speaking more personally, was only just beginning to appear and tended to be separated from the main body of the newspaper. Typically, the pieces I wrote for the *Guardian* were mainly for the Women's page which, for many years, was the only part of the newspaper where journalism appeared about issues previously marginalised and experiences previously hushed up.

Like so many women journalists and editors in that period, I was inspired by the feminist slogan, 'the personal is political' and, certainly in my case, I un-self-consciously included personal material where relevant. As Jill Tweedie is quoted as saying in Chapter 4, this was the era when women discovered that the thoughts they harboured of frustration, resentment, desire for equality were not, after all idiosyncratic feelings affecting 'only me', but actually generally held feelings reflecting social subordination. Exploring those emotions, and understanding what had given rise to them, felt like the opposite of introspective navel-gazing.

Even so, as Anna Quindlen has said (also quoted in Chapter 4), most women journalists before the 1980s sought to adopt the impersonal voice of news discourse. Before Quindlen began writing her personal column, she believed readers 'should know no more about me than my name. The reporter's job is to report, not share an experience.

No navel gazing allowed' (Quindlen 1993, p. 15). I came through a slightly different route into journalism, and never worked in a conventional newsroom, so I never felt obliged to adopt this extreme form of invisibility. Even so, the personal was not something you would necessarily foreground, particularly in newspapers, where the dominant discourse, even in feature writing, was one which was primarily research based with the journalist acting as a conduit for others' experiences and views. Of course, I sometimes included personal material but would then invariably widen out from it and, frequently, I would not include personal material at all. Writing, for example, on the Women's page of the *Guardian* about women's relationships with their mothers-in-law, I made a passing and evasive reference to my own difficult relation with my mother-in-law, but then turned to other women who agreed to be interviewed as well as psychologists and comedians, to explore this as a wider social phenomenon. It never crossed my mind to write, as one would undoubtedly be encouraged to do now, a full-blown account of what had gone wrong in my own relationship. This wasn't so much about making myself invisible, but it was a reticence about too much intimate detail in the context of a medium which largely spoke in a personality-less voice.

Anna Quindlen went on to write an Opinion Column for the *New York Times*, by which time she not only included personal material but also felt strongly that to do so was important since it allowed the lives and voices of the women she represented – working mothers – to be registered in a serious public forum. Like Quindlen, I also wrote a column on the op-ed pages (of the *Guardian* 1995–2005) and again, like her, found it by then not only natural but also important to speak personally. Indeed I felt that I had been lucky enough to get this work partly because I was able to articulate the kind of personal experiences and ways of viewing the world of politicised women. Including personal detail wasn't however confined to women's issues but more widely where relevant and where it illuminated a wider social issue. Writing about the legacy of Thatcher's sale of council housing, it seemed utterly natural to write about my own experiences of growing up on such an estate and reflecting on the changes I could observe.

Of course column writing, as explored in this book, has been one of the key areas where the personal voice, which was always present in journalism, was always more easily heard and which, since the 1980s, has been growing into an ever louder and more dominant presence in journalism. Even so, at the point where I first started writing an op-ed column, the personal voice tended to be expressed more through the individuality of opinions, through the distinctiveness of the journalistic voice and through individual style rather than the inclusion of more personal autobiographical material. To speak personally so openly was still unusual.

Since the 1980s, however, as we have seen in this book there has been an explosion of personal material and first-person journalism. This has not just been the huge expansion of more opinionated writing, now spilling beyond its demarcated pages, where the subjectivity of the journalist is obvious, but also the explosion of more personal writing and more intimate details of which confessional writing is the ultimate form. As I have argued in this book, this explosion cannot be attributed to just one cause but is the culmination of a number of social trends. Like a lake which has been slowly filled by a number of underground tributaries, this lake has been fed by various different cultural forces from disillusionment with so-called objective journalism and its hidden voice of authority, through a growing cultural need to see the person behind the views, to the increasing preoccupation with confessing, exploring and witnessing intimate feelings and reactions to life's dilemmas. Whatever the causes, the result is a huge change. In any area of journalism, other than the ever shrinking area known as news reporting, the personal voice, the personality and intimate personal material are in the ascendency. Speaking personally is what we do and what we want to hear now, and the Internet and social media are the apotheosis of these trends.

Some journalists, critics and academics recognise at least some of these cultural trends. There is, for example, huge interest in the Internet and social media and its forms of communication questioning what are the implications of these for conventional journalism. These debates often appear under the heading, 'the crisis of journalism' or 'the future of journalism'. There is also widespread recognition of the fallacies of journalism's claims to 'objectivity', often voiced in academic debates about 'political bias in journalism'. There is even discussion of the increasing focus of journalism on intimate and emotional issues, discussions which invariably take place under the heading, 'tabloidisation'. Nevertheless there is staggering lack of interest in and attention to these new sorts of journalism as journalism. Insofar as they are studied, it is as symptoms of decline and crisis, evidence of a move down market, of journalism's lack of seriousness and its inability to serve the public. In short, the focus of journalism studies is far, far narrower than the focus of journalism itself.

What are the reasons for this narrowness of interest? Two elements seem particularly significant here. One is a gender issue. I may have been talking as if feminism's battles have been won long ago, but a brief look at the dominant discourse of journalism studies reveals just how male it still is. Journalism itself may have widened its field to include a wider range of issues including health and the body, sex and childrearing, relationships and domesticity, life and death, but journalism studies still treads the same path. Even as the newsrooms shrink before their eyes, and as young audiences turn to other forms of consuming information, the flak-jacket theorists of journalism studies can't take their eyes away from their preoccupations with the coverage of disaster, war and Westminster – the old 'hard news' agenda.

The other reason is snobbery. Many of the developments outlined in this book have close associations with magazine journalism, feature writing and above all, tabloid journalism, although, as this book has made clear, such developments neither originated in tabloid journalism nor are they confined there. But journalism studies is infused with despair about 'dumbing down' by which is meant the 'tabloid' focus on human interest and individual stories at the expense of 'real' news. The human interest agenda and its potential contagion of 'serious' newspapers are seen as threatening the very basis of democracy itself, creating a nation which eschews proper political and social debate for the alleged titillation of reading about personal experiences. What lurks behind these views is an incredibly old-fashioned, and rather offensive, notion of the masses who are being denied access to serious debate and, too stupid to know better, are happy to be fobbed off with salacious material. These attitudes surfaced occasionally in the Leveson Inquiry into Press behaviour (2012). Although initially focused on the behaviour of the press in terms of law breaking or unethical behaviour, some of those called to give evidence seemed to be expressing a much more widespread concern about the human interest agenda in the press per se.

This lack of critical engagement with these new forms of journalism, on the one hand, and snobbery towards it, on the other, does have some real consequences, in particular the fact that no one knows very much about its history, its cultural roots or more importantly, how it works. Whereas most journalists and academics can trot out an account about how journalism creates impressions of objectivity and why that's an illusion, most seem happy either to ignore first-person journalism or, more bizarrely, to leave it unexplored as if there's nothing to say about the autobiographical voice because it is simply the voice of 'truth'. While there is work on the conventions of objective journalism – its tropes, its mode of address, its generic conventions – there is nothing on subjectivity. Yet, as we have seen in the course of this book, all these journalistic discourses are as heavily constructed and convention bound as objective journalism and nowhere more so than when they present themselves as the unmediated voice of personal experience in confessional journalism and blogging.

This lack of any understanding of the generic conventions shows up among contemporary journalism students. It's easy to teach them about the conventions of 'objective' news writing – absent yourself, get to the point quickly and don't use any adjectives which betray your personal position. Simultaneously, most journalism tutors insist their students must keep personal blogs if they want to get along in the new world of journalism. But as soon as students encounter feature writing where the boundaries these days are so much more unclear about the use of the first-person pronouns, everything falls apart. Students, especially those who mainly read features-based news, or have been encouraged to write blogs, know that the personal pronoun is often found there and that personal experience can count, but don't know why or when or how. As a result, many include themselves in pieces randomly or lurch from personality-less reportage to arbitrary inclusion of their views and experience. My mantra with such students has become: only include the personal when relevant, if your experiences are germane to the subject, or you are the story, or if you are specifically writing comment. The more nuanced issues, about how personal style can emerge without use of the first-person pronoun or how and when many far more experienced journalists than themselves do often write themselves into research-based reportage, usually have to wait.

It's not just the technical issues thrown up by this writing that are being neglected by this snobbery, it's also, more seriously, ethics. As this book has revealed, this new form of writing is throwing up numerous new ethical issues – from new journalism's 'imagining' of the inner life of its subjects so characteristic of contemporary American literary journalism, through questions of how journalists can protect themselves against the pressure towards self-exposure, right up to what are the limits journalists should observe when exposing their own friends and family in personal confessions. Walt Harrington in his book *Intimate Journalism, the Art and Craft of Reporting Everyday Life* (1997) makes the important point that this kind of journalism requires, 'a somewhat different ethical stance for journalists' (p. xxiv). In classical journalism, Harrington points out, it is the reader who the journalist must serve first, above those he is writing about and those he is writing for. 'Yet when writing about the intimate lives of ordinary people' he continues, 'I believe journalists must adopt a hybrid ethical outlook'. This hybrid ethical outlook, he says, would be nearer to that of the anthropologist who must do 'everything within his power to protect their physical, social and psychological welfare and to honour their dignity and privacy' (ibid.). But, he cautions, intimate journalism is even more critical because of the journalistic requirement to be factual and to tell the truth. This requirement means that wherever possible journalism will give real names and real circumstances which in turn requires new ethical behaviour towards the subjects who must be fully informed. Journalists, he says, must be completely honest about the kind of subject and the kind of story they are pursuing and they must never resort to 'ambush stories', that is when a journalist approaches a subject for an interview without giving them any warning. In addition, the journalist must explain clearly the full meaning and implications of 'on record' and 'off record'. But he concludes some of journalists' established ethics must remain especially their obligation to telling the story accurately: 'the final rule is still never to write a story that omits information to protect a subject if that information would alter a reader's basic interpretation'.

Harrington's is one of the few discussions of what can only become an increasingly complex and pressing area of concern given the trend towards ever more personal and confessional material. Some people will not agree with his suggestions or feel they don't go far enough. What, for example, should editors or journalists do when confronted with some of the extremes of exhibitionism and fakery that this kind of journalism can invite? But they do at least represent an attempt to grapple with these issues. Yet the fact that Harrington's book, written in 1997, has not produced much detailed debate or follow-up is symptomatic of the attitude I have discussed earlier. This remains a neglected, under-theorised and generally disparaged area of journalism, even though its dilemmas are sure to increase given that the wider culture is pushing generally in the direction of witnessing ever more intimate and personal experiences.

Should we lament these developments in journalism and blame them for these new dilemmas and ethical conundrums? As this book has made clear, even if we wanted to there is little that could be done to turn back the tide of such a powerful trend. Journalism is only part of something much bigger which has to do with how in a complex, individualistic society, people try to understand themselves, others and social behaviour. 'In an era when people live harried, cynical and fragmented lives, far worse than we could have imagined only a few decades ago, a journalism that honestly and accurately evokes and describes the everyday lives and interior worlds is more than a strategy for selling newspapers' says Harrington (ibid., p. xiv).

Do I regret being part of a small tributary which turned into a torrent when I tentatively included some personal snippets when writing for example about relations between women and their mothers-in-law? Far from it. Looking back on that article I wonder if I went far enough? I wonder if I might have cast more light on the subject if I had stayed with my own difficulties and had been much more personal? But, back then, I hesitated over what would happen if this was read by other members of the family. Would it make a difficult situation worse? Now I think that perhaps a deeper scrutiny of myself might have made me understand my own situation and behaviour better and perhaps cast a more illuminating light on other people's situation too, a situation which was not just about my idiosyncratic emotional life but a story of intergenerational conflict about women's roles. This is not inappropriate material for journalism. As Harrington says, 'The stories of everyday life – about the behaviours, motives, feelings, faiths, attitudes, grievances, hopes, fears and accomplishments of people as they seek meaning and purpose in their lives, stories that are windows on universal human struggle – should be at the soul of every good newspaper'.

When Harrington wrote this, the World Wide Web didn't even exist. But the Internet has precisely flourished in the space he describes. The Internet and social media are quintessentially, albeit paradoxically, personal in their mode of address and often their subject matter. Because of this, the issues and dilemmas that arise from speaking personally can only increase. As more and more people turn to these sources of information, and these types of communication, the greater is the need to understand and explore them. This book, hopefully, is the first step in that direction.

Bibliography

Allan, S. 2004. News Culture, Berkshire: Open University Press.

Allan, S. 2006. Online News: Journalism and the Internet, Berkshire: Open University Press.

Andrews, P. 2001. Who Are Your Gatekeepers? Blog at http://scripting.com/davenet/2001/03/30/whoAreYourGatekeepers.html

Arnold, M. 1871. Friendship's Garland, London: Smith and Elder and Co.

Bagehot, W. 1858. In an Article for National Review Entitled Charles Dickens and Dated (1858-10-07).

Brainbridge, C. 2009. '"They've Taken Her!" – Psychoanalytic Perspectives on Mediating Maternity, Feeling and Loss'. Studies in the Maternal 2.1.

Bauman, Z. 2001. The Individualized Society, Cambridge: Polity. ISBN 0-7456-2506-1.

Bauman, Z. 2001. Community: Seeking Safety in an Insecure World, Cambridge: Polity Press.

Beck, U. and Beck-Gernsheim, E. 2001. Individualization: Institutionalized Individualism and Its Social and Political Consequences. Vol. 13, London: Sage Publications.

Belford, B. 1986. Brilliant By-Lines: A Biographical Anthology of Notable Newspaperwomen in America, New York: Columbia University Press.

Bignell, J. 2004. An Introduction to Television Studies, Oxford: Routledge.

Bird, E. 2008. Tabloidisation in the International Encyclopedia of Communication, Oxford: Blackwell.

Braden, M. 1993. She Said What?: Interviews with Women Newspaper Columnists, Lexington, KY: University Press of Kentucky.

Briscoe, C. 2006. Ugly, London: Hodder & Stoughton.

Cameron, J. 1984. BBC Five Part Documentary Series Once Upon a Time. http://www.youtube.com/watch?v=l9tI-ZQUNsE

Capote, T. 1966. In Cold Blood. Random House, reprinted in 1994, New York: Vintage.

Chalaby, J. 1998. The Invention of Journalism, Basingstoke: Palgrave Macmillan.

Chambers, D., Steiner, L. and Fleming, C. 2004. Women and Journalism, Oxford: Routledge.

Chomsky, N. 2003. The Iraq War and Contempt for Democracy in ZNet, http://www.chomsky.info/articles/20031031.htm

Christmas, L. 1997. Chaps of Both Sexes? Women Decision-Makers in Newspapers: Do They Make a Difference? London: Women in Journalism.

Conboy, M. 2000. The Press and Popular Culture, London: Sage.

Conboy, M. 2004. Journalism. A Critical History, London: Sage.

Conboy M. 2005. 'The Print Industry – An Overview', in Print Journalism: A Critical Introduction, ed. R. Keeble, Oxford: Routledge.

Conboy, M. 2005. Tabloid Britain: Constructing a Community through Language, Oxford: Routledge.

Conboy, M. 2011. Journalism in Britain. A Historical Introduction, London: Sage.

Coward, R. 1984. Female Desire, London: Paladin Books.

Coward, R. 2005. Diana: The Authorised Portrait, London: HarperCollins.

Coward, R. 2009. 'Me, Me, Me., The Rise and Rise of Autobiographical Journalism', in The Routledge Companion to News and Journalism, ed. S. Allan, Oxford: Routledge.

Coward, R. 2010. 'Journalism Ethics and Confessional Journalism'. Journalism Practice 4.2: 224–233.

Day, A.G. and Golan, G. 2005. 'Source and Content Diversity in Op-Ed Pages: Assessing Editorial Strategies in The New York Times and the Washington Post'. Journalism Studies 6.1: 61–71.

de Waal, E. 2011. The Hare with Amber Eyes: A Hidden Inheritance, London: Vintage.

Dickens, C. 1860. Nightwalks First Appeared in All Year Round July 1860, reprinted in Dickens, C. 2010, Nightwalks London: Penguin Classics.

Didion, J. 1961. Slouching Towards Bethlehem, New York: Farrar, Straus and Giroux.

Didion, J. 2005. The Year of Magical Thinking, London: Vintage.

Duff, A.S. 2008. 'Powers in the Land'. Journalism Practice 2.2: 230–244.

Eason, D.L. 1984. 'The New Journalism and the Image-World: Two Modes of Organizing Experience'. Critical Studies in Media Communication 1.1: 51–65.

Ellis, J. 2007. TV FAQ, London: I.B. Tauris.

Ellis, J. 2009. 'The Performance on Television of Sincerely Felt Emotions'. Annals of the American Academy of Political and Social Sciences 625: 103–115.

Frank, R. 2004. 'The Trickster in the Newsroom'. Points of Entry 2.

Franklin, B (ed.). 2008. Pulling Newspapers Apart, Oxford: Routledge.

Frey J. 2003. A Million Little Pieces, New York: Random House.

Frosh, P. and Pinchevski, A. (eds.) 2009. Media Witnessing: Testimony in the Age of Mass Communication, Basingstoke: Palgrave Macmillan.

Gaber, I. 2009. Three cheers for subjectivity: Or the crumbling of the seven pillars of journalistic wisdom. Communications Law.

Gaber, I. 2009. 'Them and Us: Is There a Difference? British Journalism Review 20.1: 41–46.

Gardner, F. 2009. Far Horizons: Unusual Journeys And Strange Encounters From A Travelling Life, London: Bantam Press.

Gellhorn, M. 2005. Dachau 1945, reprinted in Cupcakes and Kalashnikovs, ed. E. Mills and K. Cochrane, London: Constable.

Gellhorn, M. 2007. In McLoughlin K. Martha Gellhorn: The War Writer in the Field and in the Text, Manchester: Manchester University Press.

Giddens, A. 1991. Modernity and Self-Identity: Self and Society in the Late Modern Age, Cambridge: Polity.

Glover, S. 1999. Secrets of the Press: Journalists on Journalism, London: Allan Lane.

Green, M.B. 2011. 'Op-Ed Issues and Authors in Regional US Newspapers'. MA Thesis, Johns Hopkins University.

Greenslade, R. 2003. Press Gang: How Newspapers Make Profits from Propaganda, London: Pan Macmillan.

Greenslade, R. 2004. Patriotism and the Media, a Lecture Sponsored by the Atkinson Charitable Foundation, http://ics-www.leeds.ac.uk/papers/vp01.cfm?outfit=pmt&folder=193&paper=1493

Greenslade, R. 2012. http://www.guardian.co.uk/media/greenslade/2012/dec/29/thetimes-national-newspapers

Grogan, J. 2008. Marley & Me Tie-In: Life and Love with the World's Worst Dog, New York: William Morrow Paperbacks.

Hampton, M. 2010. 'The Fourth Estate Ideal in Journalism History', in The Routledge Companion to News and Journalism, ed. S. Allan, Oxford: Routledge.

Harding, P. 2011. 'News and Comment: Separate Stables?' British Journalism Review 22.2: 32–38.

Harrington. W. 1997. Intimate Journalism, The Art and Craft of Reporting Everyday Life, London: Sage.

Hartsock, J.C. 2000. A History of American Literary Journalism: The Emergence of a Modern Narrative Form, Amherst: University of Massachusetts Press.

Hersey, J. 1946. Hiroshima, New York: Knopf.

Hill, A. 2005. Reality TV – Audiences and Popular Factual Television, Oxford: Routledge.

Jarvis, J. 2011. Public Parts: How Sharing in the Digital Age Improves the Way We Work and Live, New York: Simon and Schuster.

Keeble, R (ed.) 2005. Print Journalism: A Critical Introduction, Oxford: Routledge.

Keen, A. 2007. The Cult of the Amateur: How Today's Internet Is Killing Our Culture. Crown Business, Doubleday, New York: Random House.

Kerrane, K. and Yagoda B. 1998. The Art of Fact: A Historical Anthology of Literary Journalism, New York: Simon and Schuster.

Kitch, C. 1999. Great Ideas: Rethinking Objectivity in Journalism and History: What Can We Learn from Feminist Theory and Practice? American Journalism 16: 113–120.

Kramer, M. 2000. 'Narrative Journalism Comes of Age'. Neiman reports. Fall 2000 http://www.nieman.harvard.edu/reports/article/101828/Narrative-Journalism-Comes-of-Age.aspx

Lamb, L. 1989. Sunrise, London: Macmillan.

Leadbeater, C. 2009. We-Think: Mass Innovation not Mass Production, London: Profile Books.

Leveson, B. 2012. Inquiry: Culture, Practice and Ethics of the Press, published at http://www.official-documents.gov.uk/document/hc1213/hc07/0780/0780.asp

Liddle, D. 1999. 'Who Invented the 'Leading Article'?: Reconstructing the History and Prehistory of a Victorian Newspaper Genre'. Media History 5.1: 5–18.

Lippmann, W. 1921. 'Public Opinion'. 1965 Project Gutenberg 6456 http://www.gutenberg.org/ebooks/6456

Lloyd, J. 2005. 'Wanting the Bad'. The Political Quarterly 76.2: 18–19.

Lyman, R. 1998. 'Martha Gellhorn, Daring Writer, Dies at 89', New York Times, February 17, 1998.

MacLoughlin, K (2007) Martha Gellhorn: The War Writer in the Field and the Text, Manchester: Manchester University Press.

Mailer, N. 1976. Some Honorable Men: Political Conventions, 1960–1972, New York: Little, Brown.

Malcolm, J. 1990. The Journalist and the Murder, New York: Knopf.

Marr, A. 2005. My Trade, London: Pan books.

Marsh, K. 2007. 'On Impartiality'. Press Gazette, 29 July 2007.

Marzolf, M. 1977. Up From the Footnote: A History of Women Journalists, New York: Hastings House.

Mayhew, H. 1861. London Labour and London Poor (1861–62) Edition used Cosimo inc 2011. Online edition.

McNair, B. 1995. Introduction to Political Communication, Oxford: Routledge.

McNair, B. 1998. The Sociology of Journalism, London: Bloomsbury.

McNair, B. 2003. News and Journalism in the UK, London: Routledge.

McNair, B. 2008. 'I, Columnist' in Franklin, B (ed.) 2008. Pulling Newspapers Apart, Oxford: Routledge.

Miller, J. 1990. The Journalist and the Murderer, New York: Knopf/Random House.

Mills, E. and Cochrane, K. 2005. Cupcakes and Kalashnikovs: 100 Years of the Best Journalism by Women, London: Constable.

Mills, K. 1988. A Place in the News: From the Women's Pages to the Front Page, New York: Dodd, Mead.

Mindich, D.T.Z. 1998. Just the Facts, New York: New York University Press.

Miraldi, R. 1990. Muckrakers and Objectivity Journalism's Colliding Traditions, New York: Greenwood Press.

Mitchell, J.L. 1940. 'The Old House at Home'. New Yorker April 13, 1940, reprinted in McSorley's Wonderful Saloon (1943), New York: Duell, Sloan and Pearce.

Myerson, J, 2009. The Lost Child, London: Bloomsbury.

Nord, L. 2006. 'Between News and Views: The Rise of Analyses and Commentaries in News Reporting'. Paper presented at the annual meeting of the International Communication Association, Dresden International Congress Centre, Dresden, Germany, June 16, 2006.

O'Beirne, K. 2006. Don't Ever Tell: Kathy's Story: A True Tale of a Childhood Destroyed by Neglect and Fear, Edinburgh: Mainstream Publishing.

Orwell, G. 1937. 'The Spanish Civil War: Wounded by a Sniper', in Faber Book of Reportage, ed. J. Carey, London: Faber.

Pauly, J. 1990. 'The Politics of New Journalism', in Literary Journalism in the Twentieth Century, 110-ed, ed. S. Norman, New York: Oxford University Press.

Plummer, K. 2001. Documents of Life 2: An Invitation to a Critical Humanism, London: Sage.

Preston, P. 2004. 'Tabloids: Only the beginning'. British Journalism Review 15.1: 50–55.

Preston, P. 2010 & 2013. Two interviews conducted by the author in relation to research on this book.

Quindlen, A. 1993. Thinking Out Loud: On the Personal, the Political, the Public and the Private, New York: Balantine Books.

Randall, D. 2005 The Great Reporters, London: Pluto Press.

Regan, T. 2003. 'Weblogs Threaten and Inform Traditional Journalism'. Nieman Reports Harvard 57.3: 68–70.

Riley, S. 1993. The Best of the Rest: Non-Syndicated Newspaper Columnists Select Their Best Work (Contributions to the Study of Mass Media and Communications), Westport: Praeger.

Riley, S. 1998. The American Newspaper Columnist, Westport: Praeger.

Robinson, W.S. 2012. Muckraker: The Scandalous Life and Times of W T Stead, Britain's First Investigative Journalist, London: Robson Press.

Rooney, R. 1999. Think Stuff Unwanted: A History of Tabloid Newspapers in England, Unpublished manuscript. http://www.scribd.com/doc/26869993/History-of-Tabloid-Newspapers-in-England.

Rooney, D. 2000. 'Thirty Years of Competition in the Tabloid Press', in Tabloid Tales: Global Debates Over Media Studies, ed. C. Sparks and T. Tulloch, New York: Rowman and Littlefield.

Rosenbaum, R. 2002. 'Columbia's J-School Needs to Consider Trollopian Retooling'. The New York Observer, August 26, 2002.

Rosenberg, S. 2009. Say Everything: How Blogging Began, What It's Becoming, and Why It Matters, New York: Crown Publishers.

Ross, L. 1961. Portrait of Hemingway, New York: Simon and Schuster.

Rusbridger, A. 2006. 'Newspapers in the Age of Blogs' http://www.thersa.org/__data/assets/pdf_file/0011/812/RSA-Lecture-by-Alan-Rusbridger-on-newspapers-in-the-rusbridger_160306.pdf

Russell, W. H. 1854. 'The Battle of Balaclava and the Charge of the Light Brigade', reprinted in The Faber book of Reportage, ed. J. Carey, (1987) London: Faber and Faber.

Russell, W. H. 1859. My Dairy in India in the Year 1858–59, edition referred to 2010 Cambridge University Press.

Ryle, J. 1997. The Hazards of Reporting Complex Emergencies in Africa, Lecture, Nuffield College 1997. http://heinonline.org/HOL/LandingPage?collection=journals&handle=hein.journals/tlcp10&div=11&id=&page

Sala, G.A. 1859. Gaslight and Daylight, London: Arcadia and Chapman.

Santo, A. 1994. 'In Our Opinion' Editorial Page Views of Clinton's First Year'. Media Studies Journal 8.2: 97–106.

Schudson, M. 1978. Discovering the News – A Social History of American Newspapers, New York: Basic Books.

Seldes, G. 1924. The 7 Lively Arts. edition used 2001, New York: Dover Publications.

Self, W. 2001. Feeding Frenzy, London: Viking.

Shafer, J. 2003. The Fabulous Fabulists Mencken, Liebling, and Mitchell made stuff up, too. Why do we excuse them? 12 June 2003, http://www.slate.com/articles/news_and_politics/press_box/2003/06/the_fabulous_fabulists.html

Shrimsley, B. 2003. 'Columns! The Good, the Bad, the Best'. British Journalism Review 14.3: 23–30.

Silvester, C. 1997. The Penguin Book of Columnists, London: Viking.

Sims, N. 2008. True Stories: A Century of Literary Journalism, Chicago: Northwestern University Press.

Socolow, M.J. 2010. 'A Profitable Public Sphere: The Creation of the New York Times Op-Ed Page'. Journalism & Mass Communication Quarterly 87.2: 281–296.

Stephens, M.A. 2006. History of News, Oxford: Oxford University Press.

Stephens, M. 1991. 'Television Transforms the News' in Communication in History, Technology, Culture, eds. D. Crowley and P. Heyer, Society London: Pearson.

Stott, M. 1975. Forgetting's No Excuse. London: Quartet Books/Virago.

Talese, G. 1966. 'Frank Sinatra Has a Cold', in The Gay Talese Reader: Portraits and Encounters, New York: Walker and Company.

Talese, G. 2008. 'Obama's Mother' in The American Journey of President Obama, New York: Littlebrown.

Taylor, G. 1993. Changing Faces: A History of the Guardian 1956–88, London: Fourth Estate.

Thompson, H.S. 1967. Hell's Angels: The Strange and Terrible Saga of the Outlaw Motor-Cycle Gangs of California, London: Penguin.

Thompson, H.S. 1970. 'The Kentucky Derby's Corrupt and Decadent', first published in Scanlan's Monthly 1.4, reprinted in The Great Shark Hunt, Gonzo Papers, Vol. 1, Strange Tales from a Strange Time 2004, New York: Simon and Schuster.

Thompson, H.S. 1982. Fear and Loathing in Las Vegas. 1971, New York: Warner-Random House.

Tomalin, C. 2011. Charles Dickens, A Life, London: Penguin.

Tuchman, G. 1972. 'Objectivity as Strategic Ritual: An Examination of Newsmen's Notions of Objectivity'. American Journal of sociology 77.4: 660–679.

Tulloch, J. 2007. 'Charles Dickens and the Voices of Journalism', in The Journalistic Imagination: Literary Journalists from Defoe to Capote and Carter, eds. R. Keeble and S. Wheeler, Oxford: Routledge.

Tunney, S. 2009. Web Journalism: A New Form of Citizenship? Brighton: Sussex Academic Press.

Tunstall, J. 1996. Newspaper Power: The New National Press in Britain, Oxford: Clarendon Press.

Turkle, S. 1995. Life on the Screen, New York: Simon & Schuster.

Turner, G. 1999. Ordinary People and the Media: The Demotic Turn, London: Sage.

Twain, M. 1995. 'My Debut as a Literary Person', in Essays and Sketches of Mark Twain, ed. S. Miller, New York: Barnes and Noble.

Tweedie, J. 1993. Eating Children: With Frightening People (fragments), London: Viking.

Tweedie, J. 1980. It's Only Me, London: Robson Books.

Tynan, K. 1966. 'The Kansas Farm Murders' in The Critical Response to Truman Capote, ed. J.J. Waldmeir, and J.C. Waldmeir, Westport: Greenwood Press.

Vare, R. 2000. 'The State of Narrative Nonfiction Writing' excerpt from a panel discussion, 6 May, 2000. Nieman Foundation, Harvard http://www.nieman.harvard.edu/reports/article/100535/The-State-of-Narrative-Nonfiction-Writing.aspx

Wahl-Jorgensen, K. 2008. 'Op-ed pages' in Pulling Newspapers Apart, ed. B. Franklin, London: Routledge.

Walker Davies, H. (1926) The Column, New York: Knopf.

Waterhouse, K. 2007. 'Those I Have Loved and Loathed'. British Journalism Review 15.1: 7–11.

Weber, R. (ed.) 1974. The Reporter as Artist: A Look at the New Journalism Controversy, New York: Hastings House.

West, R. and Andrews, M.H.M. 1946. Black Lamb and Grey Falcon, London: Macmillan.

Williams, K. 1998. Get Me A Murder a Day: A History of Mass Communication in Britain, London: Arnold.

Wolfe, T. 1968. The Kandy-Kolored Tangerine-flake Streamline Baby, reprinted in 2005, New York: Vintage Books.

Wolfe, T. 1965. 'Tiny Mummies! The True Story of the Ruler of 43rd Street's Land of the Walking Dead', The New Yorker 11 April 1965, in Literary Journalism in the Twentieth Century, ed. N. Sims, New York: Oxford University Press, 1990: 122.

Wolfe, T. and Johnson, E.W. 1973. The New Journalism (first published in 1973), London: Picador, 1990.

Wright, K. 2012. 'Listening to Suffering: What Does Proper Distance Have to Do with Radio News?' Journalism: Theory, Practice and Criticism 13.3: 284–302.

Yasmin, A.B. 2007. In Conversation with the Author. 11 May Roehampton University.

Young, H. 2003. Supping with the Devils: Political Writing from Thatcher to Blair, London: Atlantic Books.

Zelizer, B. 2009. The Changing Faces of Journalism: Tabloidization, Technology and Truthiness, Oxford: Routledge.

Index

Adams, Tim, 104
Adie, Kate, 75
advertisers, 17, 71, 124
advertising, 44, 71, 124–6
advocacy journalism, 13, 26
Ahearn, Nan, 64
Akass, John, 46
Alibhai-Brown, Yasmin, 47, 100
Allan, Stuart, 16, 116
American journalism, 14, 43, 72
American journalists, 38, 40
A Million Little Pieces (Frey), 94
Andrews, Paul, 131
anonymity, journalists, 41, 108, 130,
    132, 133
Armies of the Night (Mailer), 58–9
Armstrong, Heather (blogger), 123–5
Arnold, Matthew, 36
Art of Fact (Dickens), 24
As I please (Orwell's column), 41
Askham, Dawn, 1–2
Askham, Iain, 1–2
autobiographical
    journalist, 6
    writing, 11, 107, 121
A Writer's Life (Talese), 65
A Year of Magical Thinking
    (Didion), 66

Babble.com, 129
Bagehot, Walter, 24, 30
Bauman, Zygmunt, 10, 89
BBC, 3, 29, 47, 75, 80, 86, 92, 115
Beaverbrook, Lord, 15, 37
Because I said so.com (Meehan's blog),
    127

Beck, Ulrich, 10, 89
Beck-Gernsheim, Elisabeth,
    10, 89
Beddlington, Emma (blogger), 130
Belford, Barbara, 26, 40, 71
Belkin, Lisa, 124–5
Bell, Matthew, 106, 107
Bennett, Catherine, 95
Bignell, Jonathan, 88
Birchill, Julie, 48–9, 104
Bird, Elizabeth, 84
bloggers, 6, 70, 113, 114, 116–18,
    120–1, 123–7, 130–1, 133
    see also individual bloggers
blogging
    confessional, 117–33
    conventional journalism vs, 52
    cyberspace, intimacy and
        universality of, 113–33
    dilemmas, 119–33
    impersonal voice, 13, 39
    status of opinion, 70
    unmediated voice of, 138
    see also Internet
Bly, Nelly, 26, 38, 71
Booth, Lauren, 109
Braden, Maria, 72
Brick, Samantha, 97
Brilliant Bylines (Belford), 71
Briscoe, Constance, 94
British journalism, 8, 13, 36, 39, 41,
    47, 70
    women's place in, 73–4
British journalists, 41, 54
Brown, Ben, 96
Buford, Bill, 28

Burchill, Julie, 48
Byatt, A. S., 107

Cairncross, Frances, 79
Cameron, James, 27–9, 41, 44
Capote, Truman, 52, 56, 59–61, 63,
   66–8
Cassandra (Connor's column), 41
Centre Daily Times, 101
Chalaby, Jean, 17
Chambers, D., 72, 73
Chomsky, Noam, 20, 45
Christmas, Linda, 77, 80, 82
Cleave, Chris, 104
Clifford, Max, 2–3
Cochrane, Kira, 78
In Cold Blood (Capote), 56, 59, 60, 61,
   66, 68
Cole, John, 42
columnists
   American, 40–1
   British, 47
   celebrities as, 49
   contemporary, 51
   national, 50
   nature of authority, 48
   newspaper, 41, 48, 49
   personal, 101
   political, 41, 47, 50
   pseudonyms, use, 41
   public prominence of, 47
   women, 72, 104–5
The Column (Davies), 39
columns
   authored, 40
   vs editorials, 36–9
   gossip, 40
   personal, 9, 39, 49, 91, 93, 97
   political, 39
comment
   columns, 35
   pages, 35, 38, 46
   writers, 35, 48
   writing, 32

commentariat, 8, 13, 47, 50
   see also columnists
composite characters, 24, 25, 54, 101
Conboy, Martin, 71, 73, 74, 82–4
confessional columns, 1, 99, 102
confessional journalism
   characteristics, 93–4
   controversies in, 96–101
   ethics in, 107–11
   real life stories in, 90–1, 94
   striking aspects of, 91
   see also blogging; conventions,
      confessional journalism
confessional journalists, 110, 120, 126
confessional society, 10, 70–90
Connor, William (Cassandra), 41
contemporary journalism, 1, 3, 23, 32,
   66, 70, 91, 97, 138
   see also real life stories
conventions, confessional journalism,
   101–7
   in America, 101
   exhibitionistic personality, 112,
      118, 121–2, 125
   faux persona, 111
   humanity of, 112
   the persona, 102, 104, 111–12, 115
   rhetorical devices, 103
   self-effacement, 102
   in UK, 101–2
Cooke, Alistair, 42, 75
Cooke, Rachel, 97, 111
Cosmopolitan, 78, 134
Coward, Ros, 79, 84, 90, 95
Cupcakes and Kalashnikovs, 74
Cusk, Rachel, 92, 110, 118
cyberspace, 113–33

Daily Express, 37, 41, 74, 83
Daily Herald, 83
The Daily Mail, 2, 11, 19, 35, 49, 85,
   92, 97, 98, 105, 106, 109
The Daily Telegraph, 25, 85, 92, 106,
   134

Day, A. G., 39
Deer Park (Mailer), 58
demarcation (newspaper sections), 15, 35
democratisation of journalism, 116–17
  see also Internet
Diamond, John, 6, 9, 103
Diary of Samuel Pepys (Pepys), 126
Dickens, Charles, 23–6, 30
Didion, Joan, 9, 11, 52, 56, 65–9
digital dis-inhibition, 130
Dix, Dorothy, 72–3
Dixie, Florence, 73
dooce com (Armstrong's blog), 123, 125
Don't Ever Tell (O' Beirne), 94
Dowler, Millie, 11
Dowling, Tim, 6, 49, 93, 102, 104, 110–111
Down with the Kids (Cleave's column), 104
d'Souza Christa, 99, 110
Duff, Alistair, 39, 47, 48
dumbing down, 8, 11, 90, 137

Eason, D. L., 67
editorials
  columns in, 36–9, 50
  commentary on, 46
  newspapers identity and, 34–6, 83
  political intervention, 34
  section, 37
  subjective voices in, 13
  tabloid type, 33
  writing style, 33
The Electric Kool-Aid Acid Test (Wolfe), 55
Ellis, John, 10, 16, 30, 84, 88
emotions, 3, 9, 20, 28, 65–6, 68, 79, 87, 89, 93, 96, 106, 112, 124, 131, 134
emotional life (subject of journalism), 54, 68, 82, 87, 88, 105, 140
Engel, Mathew, 9

Esquire, 55, 57, 63
ethical dilemmas, 7, 10–11, 59, 68, 89, 101, 119–21, 133
  inaccuracy, 29, 30–1
  misrepresentation, 68, 112
ethics, confessional journalism, 107–11
  ambush stories, 112
  dialogue, 110
  and family, 107–10
  on and off record, 107–11
  permission, 109
  representing friends, 107, 109–10
  of self-exposure, 3
exhibitionism, 11, 24, 112, 118, 121–2, 125, 139
extreme experiences, 11, 106
Eyre, Crowe, 22

Facebook, 1, 4, 24, 94, 109, 115, 121, 131
faux humiliation, 106
Fear and Loathing in Las Vegas (Thompson), 62
feature writing, 56, 90, 91, 137, 138
feauturisation, 82–7
Feeding Frenzy (Self), 85
fem-humiliation, 105, 106
feminisation of journalism, 71–81
feminism, 20, 73, 75, 77–9, 87–9, 106, 137
Fenton, James, 29
Fern, Fannie, 38
Forgan, Liz, 78
Fowler, Alys, 49
Frank, Russell, 102, 131
Frank, Ze, 115
Franklin, B., 13
Frank Sinatra Has a Cold (Talese), 63
Freeman, Hadley, 106
Frey, James, 94–5
Friedrichs, Hulda, 73
Frosh, P., 30

Gaber, Ivor, 17, 20
Gale, George, 46

Gardiner, Becky, 93, 108
Gardner, Frank, 92
A Gay Girl in Damascus (blog), 132
Gaslight and Daylights (Sala), 25
Gellhorn, Martha, 27–8, 41, 74
gender in journalism, 48, 71, 76, 80,
    81, 136
    see also feminisation of journalism,
        71–81
Giddens, Anthony, 10, 89
Glover, Stephen, 48
Golan, G., 39
Goldman, Francisco, 9
Gold, Tanya, 92, 96, 98, 104–5, 107–8
Gonzo journalism, 52–69
Goody, Jade, 3
The Great Reporters (Randall), 22
The Great Tasmanian Cargo
    (Dickens), 24
Green, M. B., 45
Greenslade, R., 37, 42, 84, 86
Grogan, John, 53
The Guardian, 4, 5, 6, 9, 10, 11, 37, 45,
    47, 49, 50, 51, 58, 77, 78, 79, 81,
    85–7, 93–4, 96–100, 102–8, 110,
    116, 118, 120–1, 123, 126, 130,
    132, 134–5
    comment and analysis, 35, 46
    family supplement, 4, 92
    op-ed section, 42–3, 46
    weekend magazine, 49, 92, 93
    Women's page, 75, 76
    writing styles, 33

Hall, Justin (blogger), 119–22, 124
Hampton, M., 17
Harding, Bert, 28
Harding, Phil, 13
hard news versus soft news, 14, 55, 81,
    87, 137
The Hare with the Amber Eyes (de
    Waal), 53
Harrington, Walt, 138–40
Hearst, 15

Hell's Angels: The Strange and Terrible
    Saga of the Outlaw Motorcycle
    Gangs (Thompson), 61
Heren, Louis, 42
Hersey, John, 54
Hetherington, Alastair, 76, 77
Hill, Annette, 88
Hiroshima (Hersey), 54
History of The Guardian (Taylor), 42
Hitchens, Peter, 47, 51
Hopper, Hedda, 73
Household Words (magazine), 25
How to Lose Friends and Alienate People
    (Young), 107
Huffington, Arianna, 113
Huffington, Michael, 113
The Huffington Post, 7, 113, 114

Illustrated London News, 26
immersion journalism, 22, 57, 61, 62,
    63, 64
impartiality, 13, 16, 18, 20, 22, 57
impersonal writing, 18
The Independent, 4, 6, 85, 106, 107
inner life of journalist, 70, 138
Inside the Madhouse (Bly)
Internet
    anonymity, 132
    confessions of bloggers, 6, 98, 114,
        116–17, 121, 123–5, 129–30
    consumption pattern and, 9
    contemporary journalism and, 1
    critics view, 14, 50
    dialogue with readers, 7
    ethical dilemmas, 11
    feelings of intimacy, 87, 94, 119–20,
        131
    personal nature of, 10, 39, 88, 133,
        136, 140
    personal voice in, 10, 39, 88, 133,
        136, 140
    sense of community in, 130, 132
    and state of the press, 8
    vs traditional journalism, 113, 118

Intimate Journalism, the Art and Craft of Reporting Everyday Life (Harrington), 138
introspection, 63, 66, 68, 79, 90, 92, 104
The inverted pyramid, 18
investigative journalism, 5, 11, 26, 94
It Seems to Me (Broun's column), 40

Jarvis, Jeff, 116
Jenkins, Simon, 47, 51
Johnson, Rachel, 106
Jones, Liz, 11, 49, 97–100, 106, 108–9, 111–12, 118, 121
  authenticity, 111
  exhibitionism, 118, 121
  fakery, 98, 100
  marriage and divorce, 106
  queen of confessional journalism, 97–8
journalism
  advocacy journalism, 13, 26
  anthropological, 61
  contemporary, 1, 3, 23, 32, 66, 70, 91, 97, 138
  democratisation of, 116–17
  as fourth estate, 17, 115
  gender in, 48, 71, 76, 80, 81, 136
  immersion, 22, 57, 61, 62, 63, 64
  intimate, 6, 59, 139
  intimate revelations in, 89, 107, 129
  intimate subjects in, 88, 100
  investigative, 5, 11, 26, 94
  literary, 12, 53–4, 65, 138
  narrative, 57, 60, 63, 71, 80, 84, 89, 99, 110, 114, 118, 121, 124, 131–2
  new, 52–69
  opinion-led, 6, 39
  online, 7, 8, 35, 48, 91, 99, 108, 110–12, 123–5, 129, 131–3
  personality-based, 6

  personal voice in, 1, 6, 7, 10, 12, 33, 52, 53, 60, 70, 71, 93, 111, 117, 135–6
  studies, 13, 136–7
  stylistic conventions, 16, 21, 26, 53, 57
  television, effect on, 10, 29, 30, 44, 47, 80–1, 84, 88, 94, 97, 104, 112
  traditional, 9, 52, 57, 113
  see also confessional journalism; objective journalism
journalistic values, 28, 96
  accuracy, 16, 19, 30, 31, 36, 52, 61
  detachment, 17, 19, 20, 21, 62, 67, 71, 96
  impartiality, 13, 16, 18, 20, 22, 57
  objectivity, 13–29
  snobbery, 24, 39, 118, 137, 138
  transparency, 30
journalists
  anonymity and, 41, 108, 130, 132, 133
  autobiographical, 6
  confessional, 110, 120, 126, *see also* bloggers
  inner life, 70, 138
  personality of, 6, 10, 18, 21–3, 28, 29, 31, 33, 35, 38–9, 44, 47–50, 53, 88, 112–13, 115, 117, 119
  personal voice, 10, 32, 34, 39, 88, 122, 133, 136, 140
  subjectivity, 1, 4, 8, 10, 13, 30, 31, 38, 52, 62, 67, 68, 70, 75, 79, 82, 88, 89, 101, 136, 137
  women, 20, 71, 72, 81, 134
Junor, John, 46

The Kandy-Kolored Tangerine-Flake Streamline Baby (Wolfe), 55–6
Keeble, Richard, 82
Keen, Andrew, 94, 129, 131
The Kentucky Derby is Decadent and Depraved (Thompson), 62

Kennedy, John F., 58
Kerrane, Kevin, 24, 29
Kettle, Martin, 50
Kitch, Carolyn, 18, 20, 21, 75
Kramer, Mark, 18

Ladies' Home Journal (Thompson),
    72–3
Lamb, Larry, 83
late modernity, 10, 89
Leadbeater, Charles, 116
leaders (editorials), 33, 35, 37, 50–1
Leibling, A. J., 53
Leith, William, 104
Lennon, Peter, 58–9
Leveson, Brian, 95
Leveson Inquiry, 3, 95, 137
Levin, Bernard, 42, 44, 47, 113
Liddle, D., 36
Liddle, Rod, 109
lifestyle sections, 72, 114
Lippmann, Walter, 40–3
    Moses of Liberalism, 41
literary journalism, 12, 53–4, 65, 138
Littlejohn, Richard, 35, 47, 51
Living with Teenagers (Myerson's
    column), 4, 93, 107, 108
Lloyd, John, 50
London, Jack, 23
London Labour and the London Poor
    *(*Mayhew)
Looking After Mother (Coward's
    column), 4, 6
The Lost Child (Myerson), 4, 107
Lott, Tim, 4, 92, 110

magazine journalism, 63, 137
Mailer, Norman, 56–9, 63, 67
Malcolm, Janet, 68
mamapundit.com (Granju's blog), 127
Manchester Guardian, 73
Mangan, Lucy, 104
Marley and Me (Grogan's memoir), 53
Marr, Andrew, 14–16, 37, 41–2, 47,
    49–50

Marrin, Minette, 4
Marsh, Kevin, 14, 20, 31
Marzolf, Marion, 72
Mayhew, Henry, 22
McCann, Kate, 3
McCann, Madeleine, 2
McNair, Brian, 7, 34–5, 86
memoirs, 10, 89, 94, 95, 129
Mencken, H. L., 40, 72
Miller, J., 69
Miller, Tanis, 129
Mills, Eleanor, 72, 74, 78
Mills, Kay, 72
Mindich, D. T. Z., 14, 17
Miraldi, Robert, 17, 26
misery memoirs, 94, 129
Mitchell, David, 6
Mitchell, Joseph, 54
Mommy blogs/Mummy blogs, 117,
    124–9
Monbiot, George, 47
Mooney, Bel, 78
Morning Chronicle, 73
Morning Post, 73
muckraking, 26, 83
Mumsnet (website), 126, 129–30
Murdoch, Rupert, 82, 83, 85
My Day (Roosevelt's column), 72
My Debut as a Literary Person
    (Twain), 23
Myerson, Julie, 4–6, 93, 99, 107–8, 112

The Naked and the Dead (Mailer), 57
narcissism, 94, 100, 118, 119, 131
narrative journalism, 57, 60, 63, 71,
    80, 84, 89, 99, 110, 114, 118, 121,
    124, 131–2
Nation, 61
new journalism, 52–69
The New Journalism (Wolfe and
    Johnson), 53
new journalists, 53, 57, 66
New Magazine, 74
New Musical Express, 48

New Society, 134
newspaper
  columns, 72, 97
  layout, 37, 42
New Statesman, 8, 50, 134
news values, 19, 20, 21, 74, 79, 80,
  82, 87
news voice, 18
New Yorker (magazine), 53, 55
New York Herald-Tribune, 40, 55
The New York Times, 10, 17, 45,
  46, 80, 81, 86, 125, 135
  op-ed pages in, 45
The Newyork World, 40
Nielson, Stephanie, 128
Night walks (Dickens), 24
Nord, L., 32
Northcliffe, Lord, 15
Northern Echo, 74

Oakes, John B., 45
O'Beirne, Kathy, 94
objective journalism
  composite characters in, 24
  criterion of, 19
  defined, 13–17
  diverse group, 52
  feminists, 78
  fundamental values of, 30
  generic conventions of, 137–8
  ideology of, 17
  negative consequences of, 101
  personal voices in, 32, 34, 136
  source motivation, 61, 92
objective voice, 32, 34, 122, 136
objectivity
  conventions of, 137–8
  fact-based journalism and, 35
  historical, 20
  ideology of, 13–14, 17–19
  impartial voice, 13, 14, 16–18, 20,
    22, 29
  literary journalism, 53
  of new journalism, 55, 59, 67

personal voice, 32, 122
philosophical fallacies, 19–21
professionalism and, 16–17
reportage and, 21–9
tabloidization of, 136
women journalists', 71, 75, 78
see also objective journalism
The Observer, 21, 30, 48, 49, 58, 60, 67,
  85, 95, 97, 98, 104, 109, 111, 112,
  118
The Old House at Home (Mitchell), 54
Old Mr Flood (Mitchell), 54
On-Broadway (Winchell's column), 40
online communities, 7, 8
online journalism, 7, 8, 35, 48, 91, 99,
  108, 110–12, 123–5, 129, 131–3
On the Record (Thompson), 72
op-ed pages, 33–6, 39, 42, 45–6, 80–1,
  99, 135
opinion
  columns, 32–51, 114
  editorials, 32–51
  personal, 8, 9, 14, 39, 47, 86, 113,
    114
  pieces, 13, 34, 37, 83, 85
opinion-led journalism, 6, 39
Orwell, George, 27, 41, 43

Pall Mall Gazette, 73
Parkin, Jill, 105, 106
Parris, Mathew, 47
Pauly, John, 56
Pearson, Allison, 92–3
The Penguin Book of Columnists, 39
Pepys, Samuel, 126, 130–1
personal columns, 9, 39, 49, 91, 93, 97
personal experience, 6, 10, 88, 91, 93,
  99, 100, 117, 135, 137, 138, 139
personality-based journalism, 6
personality of the journalist, 6, 10,
  18, 21–3, 28, 29, 31, 33, 35, 38–9,
  44, 47–50, 53, 88, 112–13, 115,
  117, 119

personal material, 6, 52, 58, 70, 90, 92, 106, 115, 135, 136
personal voice, 10, 32, 34, 39, 88, 122, 133, 136, 140
personal writing, 6, 7, 8, 10, 11, 12, 18, 31, 67, 91, 131, 136
petiteanglaise.com, 125
Phillips, Melanie, 35
phone hacking, 107
Pick, Hella, 75
Pickwick Papers, (Dickens), 23
Picture Post, 28
Pilger, John, 29
Pinchevski, A., 30
pioneerwoman.com, 127
Pizzey, Erin, 78
Plummer, Ken, 88, 89
political columnists, 41, 47, 50
Potter, Lynda Lee, 74
Press Complaints Commission, 108
Preston, Peter, 42, 44, 46, 47, 76, 78, 85, 86, 87
Princess Diana, 84
privacy, 1, 4, 5, 25, 108, 109, 110, 121, 139
professionalism, 6, 8, 14, 16–18, 20, 21, 30–1, 35, 37, 56, 71, 73, 75, 95, 96, 99, 106, 113, 116
Proops, Marge, 74
Private Eye (magazine), 11, 46, 102
Pulitzer, 15, 71–2
The Pump House Gang (Wolfe), 55

Quindlen, Anna, 72–3, 80–1, 86, 134–5

Randall, David, 22, 26
Random House, 64
readers letters, 33, 38, 42
reality TV, 88, 95
real life stories, 3, 6, 10, 62, 88, 90–2, 122
   first person, 6, 11, 136, 137
Redhead, Brian, 76

Redneck Mommy, 129
Rees-Mogg, William, 42
Regan, T., 116
reportage
   classic, 13, 22
   fact-based, 35
   first person witnessing, 10–11, 21, 94, 119, 136
   journalist's personal voice, 10, 32, 34, 39, 88, 122, 133, 136, 140
   reporter as witness, 10–11, 16, 21–4, 27, 29, 57, 60–1, 88–90, 94, 96, 101, 104, 112, 119, 126, 130–1, 136, 139
Riley, S., 38, 101, 102
Roberts, Yvonne, 100, 104, 110
Robinson, Nick, 30, 115
Robinson, W. Sydney, 30, 115
Roiphe, Katie, 65
Rook, Jean, 46, 74
   'First Lady of Fleet Street', 46
Rooney, D., 84
Rooney, R., 83
Roosevelt, Eleanor, 26, 72
Rosenbaum, Ron, 14, 130
Rosenberg, Scott, 120–1, 123
Ross, Isabel, 72
Ross, Lillian, 54
Roth, Philip, 103
Rusbridger, Alan, 7, 87, 92, 113–14, 116
Russell, William Howard, 22–3

Sala, George Augustus, 25
Salam pax blog, 116
Sanderson, Catherine (blogger), 125, 132
Schudson, Michael, 15–17, 35, 41, 43
Scotland on Sunday, 49
Second world war, 27, 37, 41, 53, 57
Seighart, Mary Ann, 102
Seldes, Gilbert, 40
Self, Will, 85, 92
Shaw, Flora, 73

She (magazine), 134
Shrimsley, Bernard, 41, 47, 50
Shriver, Lionel, 107
Silvester, C., 39, 50
Simpson, John, 29
Sims, Norman, 53–6, 58–9, 67
The sixties
  comment sections, 32, 38
  crisis of authority, 89
  exploration of consciousness, 66
  feminist revolution, 74–6
  influence of television, 30
  new journalism, 52, 55–7, 59, 64,
    66, 67, 68
  op-ed pages, 42
  opinion columns, 40, 41, 42, 44,
    45–6
Sketches by Boz (Dickens), 23
Slater, Nigel, 49
Slouching towards Jerusalem (Didion),
  56, 65
snobbery
  personal journalism, 24, 39, 118,
    137, 138
  tabloids, 84–5
social attitudes, 10, 19
social media, 115, 116, 131, 136, 140
social networking, 7, 8, 115, 116, 129
Socolow, M. J., 40, 45–6
Some Dreamers of the Golden Dream
  ((Didion), 66
Sparks, C., 82
Spectator, 41, 77
Sphor, Heather (blogger), 128
Springer, Jerry, 95
Steadman, Ralph, 62
Stead, W. T., 26, 73
stephanienelson.com (Nielson's blog),
  128
Stephens, M. A., 16–17
Stephens, M., 44
Stott, Mary, 75–6
subjective interpretation, 15, 18
subjective journalism, 8, 62, 101

subjective voice, 13, 14, 82
subjectivity
  emotional life, 88
  exploring subjectivity (Didion and
    Thompson, examples), 67–9
  foregrounding subjectivity, 67
  of journalist, 1, 4, 8, 10, 13, 30, 31,
    38, 52, 62, 67, 68, 70, 75, 79,
    82, 88, 89, 101, 136, 137
The Sun, 33, 48, 74, 82, 83, 85, 86, 92,
  117
Sunday Express, 74
Sunday Times, 4, 48, 74, 85, 92
Sweet Smell of Success (film), 40
syndication, 40–1

tabloid editorials, 33–4
tabloidisation, 82–4, 86, 136
tabloids, 2, 4, 6, 8, 32, 35, 46, 82–5
Talese, Gay, 52, 56, 63–5, 67–8
Tarbell, Ida, 26, 71
Taylor, Geoffrey, 42, 77
The Telegraph, 10, 15–16, 19, 77
television, 10, 29, 30, 44, 47, 80–1, 84,
  88, 94, 97, 104, 112
Thatcher, Margaret, 48, 84, 135
thespohrsaremultiplying.com
  (Heather Spohr's blog), 128
Thompson, Dorothy, 72–3, 81
Thompson, Hunter S., 52, 55, 56,
  61–3, 65, 67, 68
the Thunderer (nick name for *The
  Times*), 36
The Times, 6, 15–16, 22, 36–8, 42, 45,
  46, 47, 62, 65, 68, 73, 85, 87, 103,
  113
  layout, 37
  leaders, 37
  writing styles, 33
Thy Neighbor's Wife (Talese), 64–5, 68
Tiny Mummies! (Wolfe), 55
Today and Tomorrow (Lippmann's
  column), 40
To Kill a Mockingbird (Lee), 59

Tomalin, Claire, 23
Townsend, Martin, 95
Toynbee, Polly, 47, 78, 80
transparency, 19, 117
trivialisation, journalism, 8
The True Story of The Ruler of 43rd
    Street's Land of the Walking Dead!
    (Wolfe), 55
Tuchman, Gaye, 17
Tulloch, John, 23, 24
Tunney, S., 116
Tunstall, Jeremy, 47, 48
Turkle, Sherry, 132
Turner, Graeme, 84
Twain, Mark, 23, 26, 40
Tweedie, Jill, 10, 77–9, 134
twitter, 48, 97, 110, 115
Tynan, Kenneth, 60

Ugly (Briscoe), 94
Under An Olive Tree (Diane's blog),
    118, 119
Unto the Sons (Talese), 65
Utley, Tom, 107

Vare, Robert, 57
VodkaMum, 129
voyeurism, 112, 125

Wahl-Jorgensen, Karin, 34, 37, 38, 48
The Washington Post, 45
Waterhouse, Keith, 41, 49, 50, 51
Weale, Sally, 93
Weber, Ronald, 55, 56, 59, 60, 67, 68
websites, 10, 98, 116–17, 119, 124, 125
weekend columns, 103
Wells, Ida Tarbell, 71
Westminster Gazette, 74
West, Rebecca, 74

What inna namea Christ is this
    (Wolfe), 63
The White Album (Didion), 66
Whittaker, James, 46
Who are your Gatekeepers?
    (Andrews), 131
Wilby, Peter, 50
Williams, Kevin, 16
Williams, Zoe, 104, 110–11
Winchell, Walter, 40
Winfrey, Oprah, 88, 94
witnesing, 10–11, 16, 21–4, 27, 29, 57,
    60–1, 88–90, 94, 96, 101, 104,
    112, 119, 126, 130–1, 136, 139
  bearing witness in journalism,
    29, 60
  of emotional life, 88
  personal feelings and reactions, 2, 8
  reporter's, 10, 16, 21–9, 61, 96
Wolfe, Tom, 52–3, 55–7, 63, 67–8, 97
women, 74
  in British journalism, 73–4
  columnists, 72, 104–5
  feminisation, 70–87
  influence of, 82
  objective journalism and, 71, 75, 78
  journalists, 20, 71, 72, 81, 134
  representation in journalism, 20,
    79–80
women's pages, 72, 75, 101
World Wide Web, 132, 140
Wright, Kate, 30

Xu, Jinglei, 118

Yagoda, Ben, 24, 29
Young, Hugo, 8, 48

Zelizer, Barbie, 82

Printed in China